THE WHOLE DUTY OF MANKIND

THE WHOLE DUTY OF MANKIND

NOTHING NEW UNDER THE SUN

Lynette L. Barton
Cover artist: Unknown

The Whole Duty Of Mankind
Nothing New Under The Sun

Scripture quotations from various translations.
including CJB; OJB; KJV, NRSVA with permission.

ISBN: 0692321845
ISBN: 9780692321843

Printed in the United States of America

CONTENTS

DEDICATION

This book is dedicated to " **The Lost Sheep Of The House Of Yisra'el**"! Whom were carried away between 740 B.C. or 722 B.C .

Ezekiel 20:23-24
'I also raised my hand and **swore** to them in the desert that **I WOULD SCATTER THEM AMONG THE GENTILES/GOYIM and disperse them through the countries**; [24] <u>because</u> they hadn't obeyed my rulings but had <u>rejected</u> my laws and profaned my *shabbats*, and their eyes had turned toward their fathers' idols.

Jeremiah 15:1
Then YHWH said to me, "Even if Moshe (Moses) and Sh'mu'el (Samuel) were standing in front of me, my heart would not turn toward this people! **Drive them out of my sight, get them out of here!**

Jeremiah 50:6
My people have been **LOST SHEEP**. My shepherds made them go astray, turning them loose in the mountains. As they wandered from mountain to hill, they **LOST** track of where their home is.

Matthew 15:24
He said, "I was sent **ONLY** to **THE LOST SHEEP OF THE HOUSE OF ISRAEL!**"

Matthew 10:5-6
[5] These twelve Yeshua sent out with the following instructions:
"DON'T go into the territory of the Gentiles/*Goyim*, and don't enter any town in Shomron,
[6] but go rather to **THE LOST SHEEP OF THE HOUSE OF ISRAEL!**

However, by the Grace of YHWH, these **LOST SHEEP** have been awakening during the past 30 years or so and are 'exponentially' increasing in numbers! Just like YHWH said would happen!

Isaiah 11:12
He will hoist a banner for the Gentiles/*Goyim (Nations)*, assemble **THE DISPERSED OF ISRAEL, AND GATHER THE DISPERSED of Y'hudah from the four corners of the earth**.

<u>Isaiah 56:8</u>

YHWH Elohim says, he who **GATHERS ISRAELS EXILED**: "There are yet **OTHERS I WILL GATHER**, <u>**besides those gathered already**</u>."

<u>Philippians 2:13</u>

[13] For Elohim is working in you, **giving you the ' desire' and the power to do what pleases him**. = T'shuvah

Acknowledgement

A Big Todah Rabba (Thank you) to my Mother Celia Collazo Reyes who always taught me that there is indeed an Elohim (God). She laid the foundation within my soul that eventually many, many decades later   when I was in my 40's , caused me to 'diligently' seek him out and that was when Yah gave me my 'ears to hear what the Ru'ach (spirit) is saying.'!

<u>Proverbs 22:6</u>
Train up a child in the way he should go: and when he is old, he will not depart from it.
THANKS MOM!

I'd like to acknowledge the loving support of my wonderful Ishi (Husband) Robert Barton who was so very patient with my 'disappearing' into our home office for what seemed to be endless weeks and hours on end during the writing of this book. To my Ishi I say. . . Todah Rabba ! (Thank you very much) my darling!
I'd also like to thank Earlene Barton for bringing my Ishi into this world. Todah Rabba Earlene! You did a wonderful job raising my Ishi!

But "above all" I want to give thanks to Abba Yah for calling me out and giving me "ears" to hear what the Ru'ach (Spirit) is saying! Todah Rabba Eloah Yah!!!!!!!! Blessed be he.

<u>REVELATION</u>
2:7, 11, 17, 29
3:6, 13, 22

[29] The one having an "ear" let him hear what the Ruach Hakodesh says to the Kehillot (communities, assemblies).

Ken Yehi Ratzon!
(May it be Yah's Will)

PREFACE

BEFORE WE BEGIN I'D LIKE the reader to know that I have "restored" our creators' Title and Name.

Instead of God it's Elohim-pronounced: Eh-loh-heem, and instead of LORD it's YHWH or Yah, and instead of Jesus it's Y'shua.

Folks, it's time to awake from our slumber we are running out of time and "must" worship and address him in truth, the way he "commands" us to do! Consider the following. . .

(Verses paraphrased).

Exodus 3:15

. . . 'YHWH, the Elohim of your fathers, the Elohim of Abraham, the Elohim of Yitz'chak and the Elohim of Ya'akov, has sent me to you.' **This is my name forever; this is how I am to be remembered generation after generation.**

Zechariah 14:9

Then **YHWH** will be king over the whole world. On that day **YHWH** will be the only one, and **his name will be the "only name".**

Acts 4:12

. . .For there is "**no other name**" under heaven given to mankind by whom we must be saved!"

Proverbs 30:4

. . .What is **his name**, and what is **his son's name**?
Surely you know!

Exodus 20:7

[7] "Do not take the name of **YHWH** your Elohim in vain, because **YHWH** will not leave unpunished someone who uses his name "**in vain**".

<u>Isaiah 52:6</u>

Therefore "**my people** shall know my name":

More on this very important subject later, I highly recommend you read this book in the 'order' presented, each circle leads smoothly into the next, precept upon precept!

PROLOGUE

I FELT THE NEED TO write a "concise" book for those who simply cannot read for hours on end. I have made this book as compact as possible yet explosive in its message, the message has been and always will be the <u>same</u> …from the beginning of creation to eternity…Based on the following words from our Creator himself …

<u>Ecclesiastes 1:9</u>
What has been is what will be,
what has been done is what will be done,
and there is "nothing new" under the sun

<u>Genesis 17:7</u>
[7] "I am establishing <u>my covenant</u>" between me and you,
<u>Along</u> with your descendants after you,
Generation after generation, as an EVERLASTING covenant,
To be Elohim (God) for you <u>and</u> for your descendants after you.

<u>Deuteronomy 29:13-14</u>
[13 (14)] "But I am <u>not</u> making this covenant and this oath <u>only</u> with you rather,
I am making it <u>both</u> with him who is standing here with us today before YHWH our Elohim
And <u>also</u> with him who is <u>not</u> here with us today. (future generations)

<u>Numbers 15:15</u>
[15] For this community there will be the "same" law (Torah)
For you as for the foreigner living <u>with you</u>;
This is a <u>never ending (olam)</u> regulation through all your generations;
The alien (ger) is to be treated the same way before YHWH as you.

PROLOGUE

IF THIS LITTLE BOOK SEEMS 'childlike', it's because it was my intension to do so. The artwork is also extremely simple, I have done it by hand wherever possible, I wanted to communicate the simple and straightforward message of our Creator in an extremely concise and simple format that even a child can understand…after all YHWH calls us his 'children', does he not? Consider the following…

<u>Deuteronomy 14:1</u>
You are the **children** of YHWH your Elohim.

<u>Luke 18:17</u>
Yes! "I tell you that whoever does not receive the Kingdom of Elohim like a **little child** will not enter it at all!"

I personally have found at least 683 quotes "**children**" of Israel (b'nei Y'srael). I pray this little book blesses and encourages you the reader to 'diligently' investigate and search out the scriptures to find its 'true' message that has always been there from the beginning for 'those' who have ears to hear!

<u>Proverbs 25:2</u>
2 Elohim (God) gets glory from "concealing" things;
Kings get glory from "investigating" things.
2 It is the glory of Elohim (God) to "conceal" a thing;
But the honour of kings is to "search" out a matter.

Those who have ears let 'them' hear what the Spirit is saying
**Revelation
2:11, 17, 29 & 3:6,13,22**

INTRODUCTION

<u>Numbers 15:15</u>

[15] For this community there will be the 'same' law for you as for the alien living with you;

This is a permanent regulation through all your generations;

The alien is to be treated the 'same' way before YHWH

As yourselves.

Introduction

The things of YHWH are "cyclical", which is why I have chosen to present this book in "circles" because circles are never ending…just like YHWH they have no beginning and no end! Our future is behind us and our past is in front of us and vice-versa.

I then listed the verses of each circle vertically on the last page of each circle section for ease of reading. How do we know Yah's ways are cyclical? Well, take a look at just a few verses…

Revelation 1:8

I am the Alef and the Tav (alpha and omega), the first and the last…

Ecclesiastes 1:9

What has been is what will be, what has been done is what will be done, and there is nothing new under the sun.

Isaiah 46:10

Declaring the end from the beginning, and from ancient times the things that are not yet done (future times), saying, MY counsel shall stand, and I will do all my pleasure.

Ezekiel 1:16

The appearance of the <u>wheels</u> and their work was like unto the colour of a beryl: and they four had one likeness: and their appearance and their work was as it were a "wheel within a wheel."

Are you getting a "circular" feeling yet? Dear reader, don't ever let 'anyone' tell you that there is 'anything new' with YHWH, because that is the biggest lie ever told by the father of ALL lies! After all doesn't it all begin and end in the Garden? We began in the Garden and our goal is to "return" (t'shuvah) to the Garden!

Make me know 'your' ways, YHWH teach me 'your' paths
Psalm 25:4

INTRODUCTION

Before we get started I want you to know you will come across a few Hebrew words or terms and so I have included a small glossary at the end of this book to 'magnify' your understanding.

<u>Zephaniah 3:9</u>
For then will I 'restore' to the people a safah berurah (pure language, purified lip), that they may all call upon the "Name of YHWH", to serve Him with shekhem echad
(one shoulder, one accord).

And so dear reader I pray this little book broadens your understanding of the 'simple' message of the Scriptures. So please enjoy and share your increased knowledge with others. The brother of The Messiah penned the following…

<u>James 1:5</u>
Now if any of you lack wisdom, let him ask Elohim, who gives to all generously and without reproach; and it will be given to him.
(<u>1 Kings 3:9 - 10</u>; <u>Proverbs 2:3-6</u>; <u>Psalm 51:6</u>; <u>Daniel 1:17</u>; <u>2:21</u>)

<u>James 1:25</u>
But if a person looks 'closely' into the **perfect** *Torah*, which gives freedom, and continues, becoming 'not a forgetful hearer' but a 'doer' of the work it requires, **then** he will be blessed in what he does.

So let's get started with the first circle…

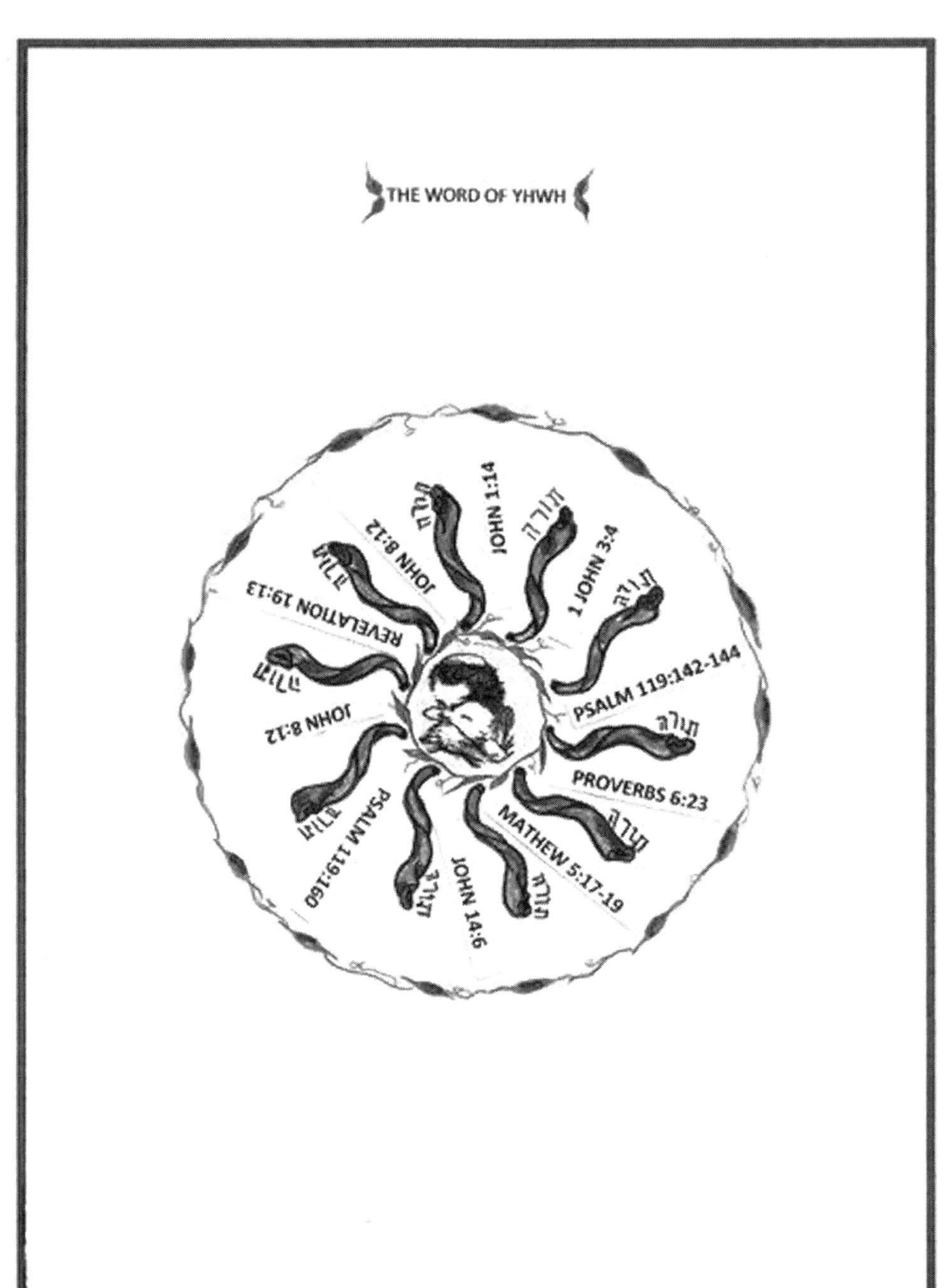
JOHN 1:14
יהוה
1 JOHN 3:4
יהוה
JOHN 8:12
יהוה
REVELATION 19:13
יהוה
PSALM 119:142-144
יהוה
JOHN 8:12
יהוה
PROVERBS 6:23
יהוה
PSALM 119:160
יהוה
MATHEW 5:17-19
יהוה
JOHN 14:6
יהוה

THE WORD OF YHWH

AS SEEN IN THIS CIRCLE, according to scripture the WORD of YAH is YAH! His WORD is his COVENANT, his WORD is Messiah and his WORD is ETERNAL! Therefore this WORD isn't just ink written on paper, this WORD is a being…an <u>Eternal</u> being!

Sadly almost the entire population on earth will tell you there is no divine law (Torah)…

Christianity outright teaches millions that the very commands of YHWH, written by HIS own finger onto stone no less and given to ALL through HIS servant Mosheh (Moses), has been done away with and nailed to the 'cross'. And so now we can have shrimp cocktail with a ham sandwich and throw away everything that YHWH himself says is ETERNAL…EVERLASTING!

To these I ask… What part of "Forever" is it you do not understand?

Because according to scripture HIS WORD is EVERLASTING. So if his ways are everlasting - how can 'anything' be done away with?

<u>Understand, scripture says:</u>

Elohim (God) <u>himself</u> is the WORD (John 1:1)

the WORD is TRUTH (PSALM 119:160)

TRUTH is TORAH (Psalm 119:142-144),

TORAH is LIGHT (Proverbs 6:23),

the WORD (Torah) became flesh (John 1:14) = (Messiah, the walking talking Torah)

Y'shua said I AM the LIGHT (Torah) of THE WORLD (John 8:12) he wasn't talking about a light bulb!,

Y'shua said "I did "NOT" come to do away with Torah/myself (Mathew 5: 17),

Sin is the transgression of Torah (1 John 3:4)

The WORD of Elohim (Revelation 19:13)

So when we see the terms: WORD, LIGHT, TRUTH, COVENANT, the WAY, MY instruction, TORAH: These all equal Elohim/Messiah, you cannot separate them! They cannot and do not 'contradict' each other. It is Biblically impossible! Because they are ONE (echad)!

EVERLASTING Covenant: Genesis 9:16; 17:7,13,19 Leviticus 24:8 Numbers 25:13 2Samuel 23:5 1Chronicles 16:17 Psalm 105:10 Isaiah 55:3; 61:8 Jeremiah 32:40 Ezekiel 16:60; 37:26 Hebrews 13:20…and many many more…

> Verily, verily I say unto you, He that Sh'ma (hear AND do) my WORD (Torah),
> "and" believeth on HIM (YHWH) that sent me, hath everlasting life, and shall not come into condemnation; but is passed from death unto life.
> **John 5:24**

CIRCLE VERSES: THE WORD OF YAH

Psalm 119:142-144 Your righteousness is eternal righteousness, and **your *Torah* is truth.**
  Trouble and distress have overtaken me, but your *mitzvoth (commands)* are my delight.
  Your instruction **(TORAH) is righteous forever**; give me understanding, and I will live.

Psalm 119:160 The main thing **about your word (Torah) is that it's true**; and all your just rulings last **forever**.

Proverbs 6:23 For the *mitzvah* (command) is a lamp, ***Torah* is light**, and reproofs that discipline are "the way to life".

John 1:14 The Word **(Torah) became a human being** and lived with us, and we saw his *Sh'khinah*, the *Sh'khinah* of the Father's only Son, full of grace and truth (Torah).

John 8:12 Y'shua spoke to them again: "I am the light (Torah) of the world; whoever follows me will never walk in darkness (Torahlessness) but will have the light **(Torah) which gives life**."

1 John 3:4 Everyone who keeps sinning is violating (*Torah*) — indeed, **sin is violation of *Torah*** (Messiah Y'shua) = Biblical wickedness.

Matthew 5:17-19 "Do NOT think that I have come to abolish the ***Torah*** or the Prophets. I have come NOT to abolish but to make it full (Magnify). [18] Yes indeed! I tell you that **until heaven and earth pass away**, not so much as a *yud* or a stroke will pass from the ***Torah*** — not until everything that must happen has happened. [19] So 'whoever' disobeys the least of these *mitzvot* and teaches others to do so will be called the 'least' in the Kingdom of Heaven. But whoever obeys them and so teaches will be called 'great' in the Kingdom of Heaven. **= Isaiah 42:21** YHWH is well pleased for HIS righteousness' sake; he will **"magnify" the Torah**, and make it honourable.

Revelation 19:13 He was wearing a robe that had been soaked in blood, and the name by which he is called is, "**THE WORD OF ELOHIM**."

My prayer dear reader, is that you 'hear' what the Ru'ach (Spirit) is saying.
Revelation 2:17

The Lamb of God

THE SEH (LAMB) OF ELOHIM (GOD)

WHO OR WHAT IS THE Lamb of Elohim? The first mention of a Lamb in scripture <u>seems</u> to be in Bereshis (Genesis) 21:28 And Avraham set apart seven ewe "lambs" of the tzon (flock) by themselves.

However I believe the very first time a Lamb was mentioned in scripture was in Genesis 3:21 YHWH Elohim, made garments (coverings) of <u>skin</u> for Adam and his wife and covered (atoned) them.

You see in Hebrew the word for 'coverings' is Kippurim, as in Yom Kippurim (Day of coverings/atonements). We see in Genesis 3:21 that 'something' was slaughtered in order to make the "covering" (atonement) of <u>skin</u> for them!... And I believe it was a Lamb not just any Lamb but THEE LAMB … Y'shua! Rev 13:8… the Lamb "slain from the foundation of the world".

Are you seeing the pattern?... Ecclesiastes 1:9 What has been is what will be, what has been done is what will be done, and there is "nothing new" under the sun.

Hebrews 9:22

In fact, according to Torah, almost everything is purified with blood; indeed, without the shedding of blood there is NO forgiveness (atonement) of sins.

Isaiah 53:7 = John 9:10

Though mistreated, he was submissive —he did not open his mouth. Like a **Lamb** led to be slaughtered, like a **sheep** silent before its shearers, he did not open his mouth.

Revelation 5:6

A **Lamb** that appeared to have been 'slaughtered'…

Revelation 13:8

And all that dwell upon the earth shall worship him, whose names are not written in the book of life of **the Lamb** "slain from the foundation of the world".

Think how much worse will be the punishment deserved by someone who has trampled underfoot the Son of Elohim;
Who has treated as something common the blood of the "covenant" which made him holy;
and who has insulted the Spirit, giver of Elohim's grace!
Hebrews 10:29

CIRCLE VERSES: THE LAMB OF YAH

Genesis 3:21 *YHWH,* God, made garments (kippurim, atonement) of skin for Adam and his wife and clothed (kippur, atoned) them.

Genesis 22:8 Avraham replied, "Elohim will provide "**himself** "the **LAMB** for a burnt offering, my son"; and they both went on together.

Exodus 12:3 Speak to all the assembly of Isra'el and say, 'On the tenth day of this month, each man is to take a **LAMB** or kid for his family, one per household.

Ezekiel 46:13 'You are to provide a **Lamb** in its first year that has no defect for a daily burnt offering to *YHWH*; do this each morning.

Isaiah 53:7 Though mistreated, he was submissive —he did not open his mouth. Like a **Lamb** led to be slaughtered, like a **sheep** silent before its shearers, he did not open his mouth.

John 9:10 So Pilate said to him, "**You refuse to speak** to me? Don't you understand that it is in my power to set you free or to have you executed on the stake?"

Revelation 5:6 Then I saw standing there with the throne and the four living beings, in the **circle** of the elders, a **LAMB** that appeared to have been slaughtered. He had seven horns and seven eyes, which are the seven fold spirirt of Elohim sent out into all the earth.

Jeremiah 11:19 But I was like a tame **Lamb** led to be slaughtered; I did not know that they were plotting schemes against me —"Let's destroy the tree with its fruit; we'll cut him off from the land of the living, so that his name will be forgotten."

Revelation 14:1 Then I looked, and there was the **Lamb** standing on Mount Tziyon; and with him were 144,000 who had his name and his Father's name written on their foreheads.

Revelation 5:8 When he took the scroll, the four living beings and the twenty-four elders fell down in front of the **Lamb**. Each one held a harp and gold bowls filled with pieces of incense, which are the prayers of Elohim's people;

Revelation 22:3 no longer will there be any curses. The throne of Elohim and of the **Lamb** will be in the city, and his servants will worship him;

I am the Alef and the Tav the First and the Last,
The Beginning and the End.
Revelation 1:8, 11 & 21:6

THE GOD OF ISRAEL!

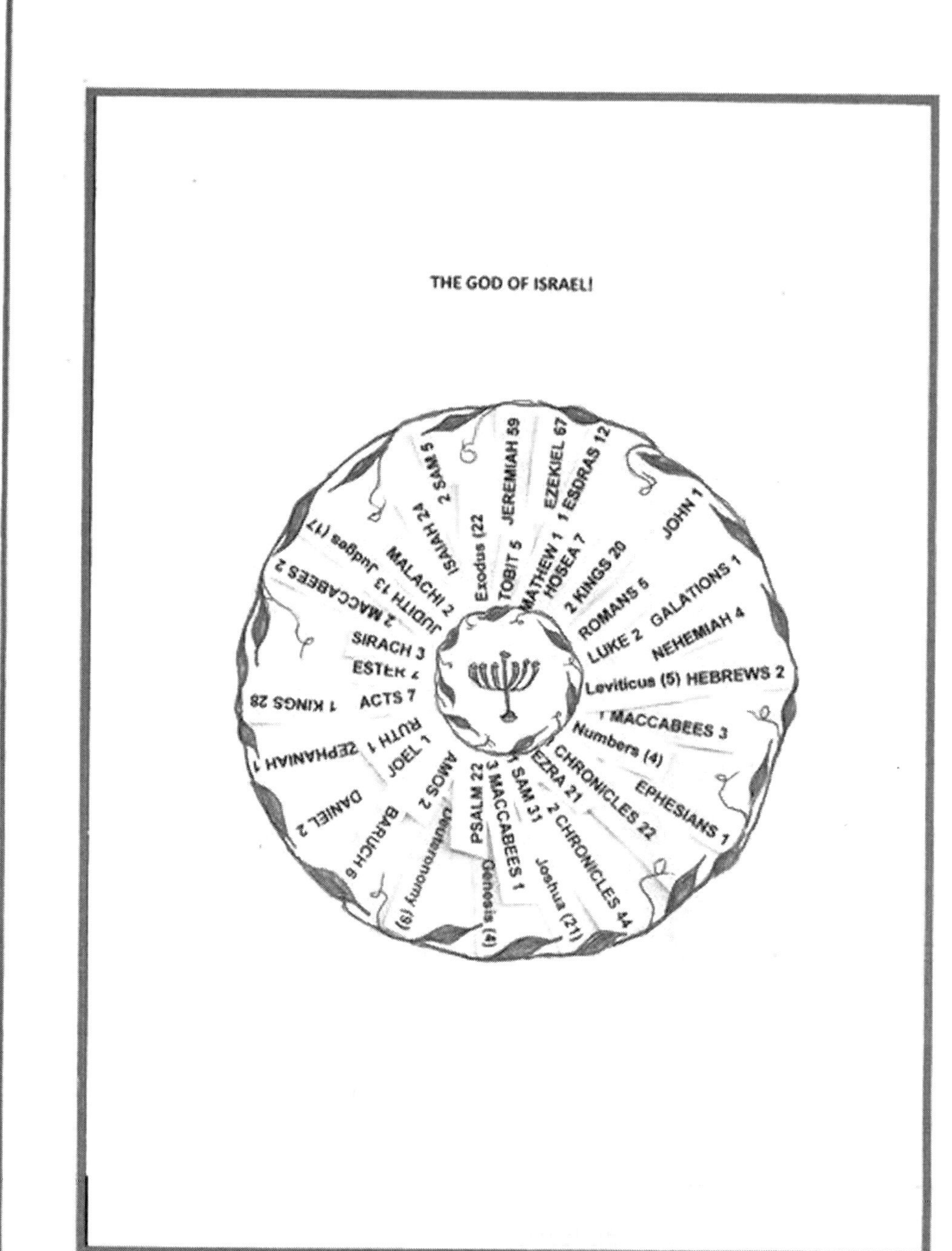

The Elohim (God) Of Y'srael

Is YHWH the Elohim of everyone? As you will discover the scriptures declare from cover to cover that he is 'exclusively' the Elohim of "Y'srael". As you can see in this circle I have found at least 515 verses declaring he is the Elohim of Israel and not in the circle are 47 versus declaring himself "the Holy one of Israel" and 80 versus declaring that "Israel" are HIS people, for a total of 642 verses declaring ONLY Israel as HIS people and HE their Elohim! Nowhere does he ever say he is the Elohim of anyone else. While it is true he is the creator of us ALL… yet he declares himself to be the Elohim of Y'srael.

This is <u>vital</u> to understanding the "redemptive" plan of YHWH. Because according to scripture… ALL of Y'srael will be saved… period! It doesn't say all the world will be saved it simply says Y'srael will be saved.

I truly believe that it is NO coincidence you the reader are reading this at this time… at this very moment in your life, I believe it is the spirit of YHWH calling you out to T'shuvah (return to HIM).

Ezekiel 36:27
I will put my Spirit inside **you** and **cause you** to live by **my (Torot) laws**,
respect my rulings and **obey them**.

Joel 4:16
[16] YHWH will roar from Tziyon, he will thunder from Yerushalayim,
the sky and the earth will shake. But YHWH will be a refuge **for his people,** a stronghold **for
the people of Isra'el.**

So please take a "close" look at the versus in this circle and know that YHWH calls himself "The Elohim of Israel" and "The Holy one of Israel" and says that "Israel" are HIS people.

Psalm 78:1-2 (Y'shua spoke in parables!)
Listen, my people, to my Torah (teaching);
turn your ears to the words from my mouth.
I will speak to you in "parables"
and explain mysteries from days of old.

<u>CIRCLE VERSES: T</u>HE <u>GOD</u> OF <u>I</u>SRAEL

503 verses declare "The GOD of Israe"!

Genesis (4)
Exodus (22)
Leviticus (5)
Numbers (4)
Deuteronomy (9)
Joshua (21)
Judges (17)
Ruth (1)
1 Samuel (31)
2 Samuel (5)
1 Kings (28)
2 Kings (20)
1 Chronicles (22)
2 Chronicles (44)
Ezra (21)
Nehemiah (4)
Psalm (22)
Isaiah (24)
Jeremiah (59)
Lamentations (1)
Ezekiel (67)
Daniel (2)
Hosea (7)
Joel (1)
Amos (2)
Zephaniah (1)
Malachi (2)
Mathew (1)
Luke (2)
John (1)
Acts (7)
Romans (5)
Galatians (1)
Ephesians (1)
Hebrews (2)
Tobit (5)
Judith (1)
Greek Ester (2)
Sirach (3)
Baruch (6)

1 Esdras (12)
2 Esdras (2)
1 Maccabees (3)
2 Maccabees (2)
3 Maccabees (1)

47 verses declare he is "The holy one of Israel":

<u>Shemot (2)</u> Exodus
<u>Vayikra (2)</u> Leviticus
<u>Bamidbar (4)</u> Numbers
<u>Devarim (1)</u> Deuteronomy
<u>Melachim Bais (1)</u> 1 Kings

<u>Yeshayah (28)</u> Isaiah
<u>Yirmeyah (2)</u> Jeremiah
<u>Yechezkel (2)</u> Ezekiel
<u>Hoshea (1)</u> Hoshea
<u>Tehillim (4)</u> Psalms

80 verses declare Israel are HIS people:

<u>Exodus (4)</u>
<u>Leviticus (1)</u>
<u>Numbers (2)</u>
<u>Joshua (1)</u>
<u>Judges (2)</u>
<u>1 Samuel (6)</u>
<u>2 Samuel (6)</u>
<u>1 Kings (7)</u>

<u>1 Chronicles (6)</u>
<u>2 Chronicles (3)</u>
<u>Ezra (1)</u>
<u>Psalm (4)</u>
<u>Isaiah (2)</u>
<u>Jeremiah (8)</u>
<u>Ezekiel (15)</u>
<u>Daniel (1)</u>

<u>Hosea (1)</u>
<u>Joel (2)</u>
<u>Amos (4)</u>
<u>Zephaniah (1)</u>
<u>Matthew (1)</u>
<u>Romans (1)</u>
<u>Hebrews (1)</u>

For a total of 630 verses!

If you profess to believe in YHWH, the Elohim of Abrahm,
Y'tzak and Yaakob, and do NOT consider yourself an Israelite,

Then it is this writers' conviction you do not understand the scriptures. . .
I pray you - the reader run after YHWH's Torah (truth) with all your strength, mind and soul.
'Only' then will he teach you HIS ways.

Shalom be with you always. . . **L.B.**

WHO IS YISRA'EL ?

Who Is Y'srael?

THE SCRIPTURES MAKE IT VERY clear that "Whom so ever" makes the decision to love YHWH with all his heart AND T'shuvah (return) AND walk in his ways (Torah)… These are his people **Israel**!

Firstly let's understand that the word gentile is "goy" in Hebrew and simply means heathen; nation; pagan; a person or nation having NO relationship with YHWH.

Ephesians 2:11-12 (Biblical definition of a Gentile)

[11] Therefore, remember your "former" state: **you Gentiles** by birth — called the Uncircumcised by those who, merely because of an operation on their flesh, are called the Circumcised — [12] at that time had no Messiah. **You were 'estranged' from the national life of Isra'el. You were 'strangers' to the covenants embodying Elohim's promise. You were in this world 'without' hope and 'without' Elohim.**

Therefore the term "believing gentile (heathen)" is an oxymoron, there is no such thing, it is impossible! You are either a heathen or you are Israel! This is what scripture says from cover to cover!

Question: Do you still want to call yourself a "Gentile"?

You see no matter who you are, or where you come from… **IF** you T'shuvah (turn away) from YOUR ways and follow Yah's ways **THEN** you are no longer a gentile (heathen, pagan) NOW you are **Israel**!

It is VERY clear in scripture there are only two types of people in this world, Gentiles (not his people) and Israel (his people).

From the beginning, if Adam and Havah (Eve) were punished (exiled) for breaking the covenant (Torah), what makes you think you can break Torah (covenant) without consequence? This is why we find ourselves where we are and don't even know WHO we are

Hear, oh earth! I am going
To bring disaster on this people; it is the 'consequence'
of their own way of thinking; for they pay no attention to my words;
and **as for my Torah, they reject it**. (Nailed to the cross nonsense!)
Jeremiah 6:19

CIRCLE VERSES: WHO IS YISRAEL: (PARAPHRASED)

Exodus 12:38 A <u>mixed</u> crowd (foreigners) also went up with them (12 tribes of **Israel)**,

Romans 11:17 You, a gentile (pagan) were grafted and are NOW **Yisraelites**!

Isaiah 56:6 And the "foreigners" who join themselves to YHWH to serve him, to love the "name" of YHWHi, and to be his workers, 'all who keep Shabbat (Sabbath)' and do not profane it, and hold fast to my covenant (Torah)…

Ephesians 2:19 so then, you are 'no longer foreigners/gentiles'. On the contrary, you are fellow-citizens with Elohim's people and members of Elohim's family (**Israel**)

Ruth 1:16 your people will be my people and your Elohim will be my Elohim. = (T'shuvah)

Matthew 15:24 He said, "I was sent **only** to the lost sheep of the **House of Isra'el.**"

Zechariah 2:15 (11) When that time comes, many Goyeem (gentiles) will join (engraft) themselves to YHWH = they become as a native born, **Israel**

Dear reader, it is my conviction that you must regard yourself as a descendant of one of those who departed Egypt in that first exodus and regard yourself as an **Israelite**… because that is how YHWH sees it! He said it and that settles it!

So that they will live by **my regulations**,
Obey my rulings and **act** by them.
Then they will be **my people**, and I will be their Elohim.
Ezekiel 11:20

May he make his face to shine upon you…Shalom **L.B.**

ONLY ISRAEL WILL BE SAVED!

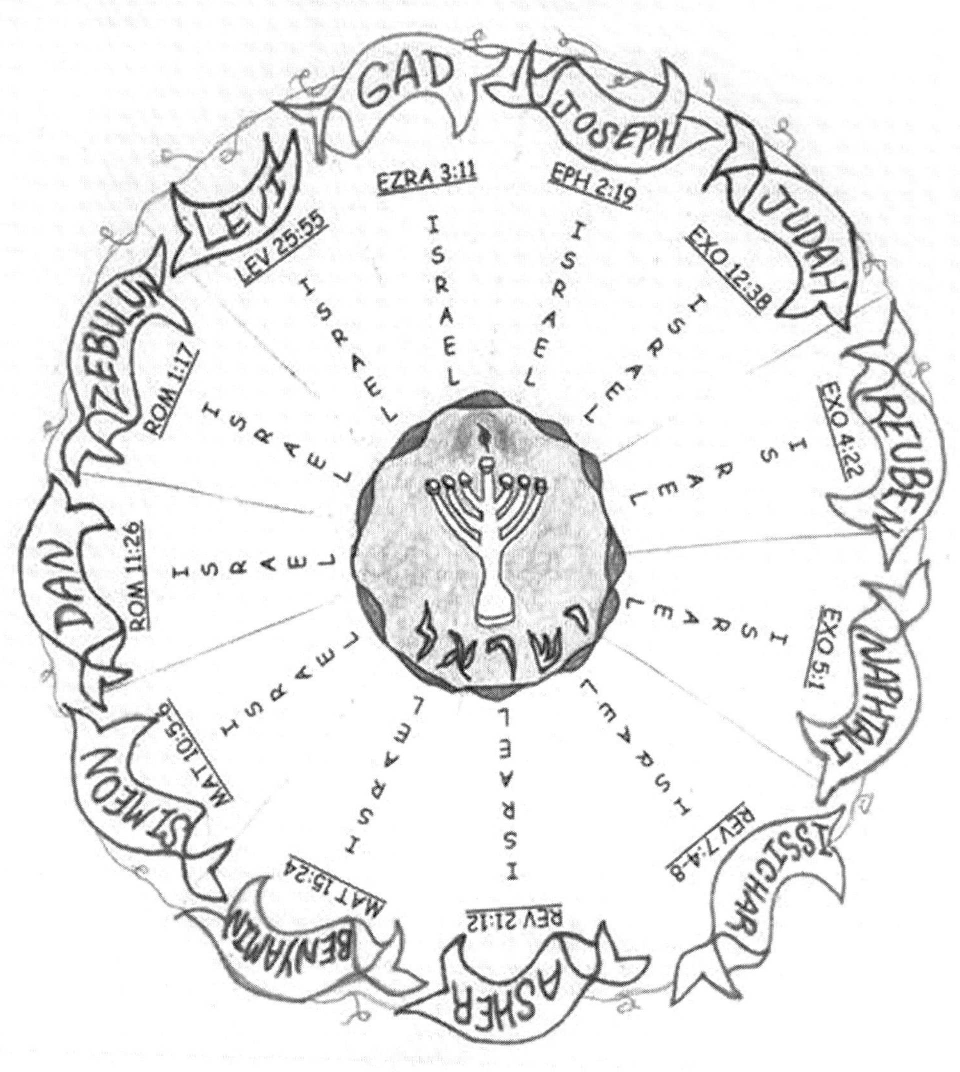

Only Israel Will Be Saved

THIS CIRCLE TELLS WHO WILL be with YHWH for ALL eternity, they are those who keep his Torah "AND" the faith of Y'shua Mashiach (Messiah),

Revelation 14:12
This is when perseverance is needed on the part of "Elohim's people", those who observe his commands (Torah) "**AND**" exercise Yeshua's faithfulness.

Revelation 12:17
The dragon was infuriated over the woman and went off to fight the rest of her children, those who obey Elohim's commands **"AND"** bear witness to Y'shua.

Did you notice there are "TWO" requirements? Just proclaiming we believe and making an altar call does NOT redeem much less 'save' anyone, it never has and it never will that is ridiculous! If that were the case Y'shua would not have had to suffer the death he did. Let's see what the brother of Messiah told us:

James 2:20
But, 'foolish' fellow, do you want to be shown that such faith "**apart**" from actions is barren?

James 2:19
You believe that "Elohim is one"? **Good for you! The demons believe it too —** the thought makes them shudder with fear!

Do you hear his sarcasm? So if the demons "believe" then why aren't they saved?

Because they reject Torah (Truth) and in doing so they reject YHWH and Mashiach. In other words, you can't just say and think you "believe", you must demonstrate that you believe through action by "doing" all the things YHWH told us to do via Mosheh (Moses) and not do what "seems" right in our own eyes!

A perfect example is the "Golden Calf" incident in the wilderness, they said tomorrow is a 'festival' to YHWH! Deut 32... remember? The people got tired of waiting for Mosheh to return and so they decided to 'worship' and 'praise' YHWH in the way they learned in Egypt. In their minds they weren't denying YHWH, they wanted to honour him in the only way they knew (inherited), the way of the heathen (gentiles), in this case the Egyptians. Three thousand lost their lives because of it that day!

That was an example for us! Are you worshipping YHWH the way the heathen (gentiles) do? Does Xmas and Ishtar (Easter) ring a bell?

Remember what YHWH told us through HIS nevi (prophet):

Jeremiah 10:2-5
"Don't learn the way of the *Goyim (gentiles; heathen),*"
…**They cut down a tree** in the forest; a craftsman works it with his axe;
⁴ **they deck it with silver and gold**. They fix it with hammer and nails,
so that it won't move.

Do you remember the xmas carol… "Silver and Gold"? How much clearer can he possibly be? This (decorating a tree) is an "abomination", this is 'mixing' good with evil. The mixing of good with evil is what caused the fall of our first parents: Adam and Havah (Eve), remember what YHWH told them?

Genesis 2:17
Except the tree of the knowledge of "good **and** evil". You are not to eat from it, because on the day that you eat from it, you will certainly die."

Most people think that all you need to do is be nice and treat others well, while that is "partly" correct the scriptures paint a far different picture! Remember the "calf" incident? They 'thought' they were doing the right thing they 'thought' they were honouring YHWH they didn't see any harm in worshipping him with a 'golden' calf, it was made of gold it was beautiful and fun!

Now that we know WHO Israel is and that there are only two people groups in this world, gentiles (heathens) and Israel. It is painstakingly obvious that out of these two groups there is ONLY one that can possibly be chosen by YHWH to enter his kingdom and spend eternity with him…it will be those who CHOOSE life! **Y'srael**! But don't believe me, believe YHWH:

Deuteronomy 30:19
"I call on "heaven and earth" to witness against you today that I have presented you with life (Torah) and death (No Torah), the blessing and the curse. Therefore, choose life, so that you will live, you and your descendants,

Hosea 4:6 (knowledge = Torah)
My people are destroyed for want of knowledge (**Torah**).
Because you rejected knowledge (**Torah**)
I will also reject you as Cohen (priest) for me. Because you forgot the **Torah** of your Elohim,
I will also forget your children.

Psalm 119:153
Look at my distress, and rescue me,
for I do NOT forget your **Torah.**

Psalm 13:4
Look, and answer me, YHWH my Elohim!
Give light (**Torah**) to my eyes, "or" I will sleep the sleep of death.

Deuteronomy 32:46-48
[46] he said to them, "Take to heart all the words of my testimony against you today, so that you can use them in charging your children to **be careful to obey "ALL" the words of this Torah.** [47] For this is not a trivial matter for you; on the contrary, **it is your life!** 'Through' it you will live long in the land you are crossing the Yarden to possess."

Dear Reader, My intent is to encourage you to "investigate" the word of YHWH and to NOT take it lightly, take it to heart…

May YHWH light your path and give you Shalom (completeness)… **L.B.**

CIRCLE VERSES: ONLY ISRAEL WILL BE SAVED

Exodus 5:1 After that, Moshe and Aharon came and said to Pharaoh, "Here is what *YHWH*, the **Elohim of Isra'el**, says: '**Let my people (Israel)** go, so that they can celebrate a festival in the desert to honor me.'"

Exodus 4:22 Then you are to tell Pharaoh: 'YHWH says, **"Isra'el is my firstborn son**.

Exodus 12:38 A "mixed" crowd (gentiles) also went up with them (**Israel**- 12-Tribes), as well as livestock in large numbers, both flocks and herds. (These ENTIRE people = **Israel**; the pagans engrafted themselves)

Romans 11:17 But if some of the branches were broken off, and you — a wild olive (gentile/heathen) — were grafted in among them (**Israel**) and have 'become' equal sharers in the rich root of the olive tree (**Israel**), (you are NOW **Israel**, 'no longer a gentile/pagan'.

Romans 11:26 and that it is in this way that ALL **Isra'el will be saved**. As the *Tanakh* (Torah, Prophets and Writings) says, "Out of Tziyon will come the Redeemer; he will turn away ungodliness (Torahlessness) from Ya'akov (**Israel**)

Ephesians 2:19-20 So then, you are 'no longer foreigners and strangers (gentiles)'. On the contrary, you are fellow-citizens with **Elohim's people (Israel)** and members of Elohim's family (**Israel**). [20] You have been built on the foundation of the emissaries and the prophets, with the cornerstone being Y'shua the Messiah himself.

Matthew 10:5-6 these twelve Yeshua sent out with the following instructions: "**Do NOT go into the territory of the Goyim (gentiles)**, and don't enter any town in Shomron, [6] but **go rather to the lost sheep of the house of Isra'el.**

Matthew 15:24 He said, "I was sent ONLY to the lost sheep of **the house of Isra'el**."

Joel 4:16 [16] YHWH will roar from Tziyon, he will thunder from Yerushalayim,
    the sky and the earth will shake. But YHWH will be a refuge for **his people**, a stronghold for **the people of Isra'el.**

Revelation 7:4-8 I heard how many were sealed — 144,000 from every tribe of the **people of ISRA'EL!**

From the tribe of Y'hudah 12,000
From the tribe of Re'uven 12,000
From the tribe of Gad, 12,000
From the tribe of Asher 12,000
From the tribe of Naftali 12,000
From the tribe of M'nasheh 12,000
From the tribe of Shimon 12,000
From the tribe of Levi 12,000
From the tribe of Yissikar 12,000
From the tribe of Z'vulun 12,000
From the tribe of Yosef 12,000
From the tribe of Benyamin 12,000

No mention of gentiles! Why? Because they engrafted themselves and are now **ISRA'EL**!

Revelation 21:12-13 It had a great, high wall **with 'twelve' gates;** at the gates were twelve angels; and inscribed on the gates were the names of the **twelve tribes of ISRA'EL.** [13] There were three gates to the east, three gates to the north, three gates to the south and three gates to the west.

No mention of gates for the Gentiles! Why? Because ONLY **ISRA'EL** is saved!

Ezra 3:11 they sang antiphonally, praising and giving "thanks to *YHWH* ", for he is good, for his grace continues forever toward **"ISRA'EL"**. All the people raised a great shout of praise to *YHWH*, because the foundation of the house of *YHWH* had been laid.

Leviticus 25:55 for to me **the people of ISRA'EL** are (evedim) (slaves; servants) they are my servants whom I brought out of the land of Egypt; I am YHWH your Elohim.

THE DAY OF YHWH
Isaiah 13:6 = Destruction !
Isaiah 63:1-6 = Vengeance & Anger !
Jeremiah 46:10 = Vengeance !
Ezekiel 13:5 = Battle & War !
Joel 1:15 = Destruction !
Joel 2:11 = Very Terrible !
Joel 2:31 & Acts 2:20 = Sun Darkened + Blood Moon !
Amos 5:18 = Darkness !
Zephaniah 1:14 = Bitter Crying !
Malachi 4:5 = Dreadful !
1 Corinthians 5:5 = Destruction of the Flesh !
2 Peter 3:10 = The Elements Melt !
Revelation 14:14-20 = Blood, Fury, Wrath !
Revelation 19:11-15 = Furious Rage, Gods Battle

THE DAY OF YAH!

WE HAVE ALL HEARD IT said that the Day of the LORD (YHWH) is Sunday or it's the millennium or it's this day or that day. However when Scripture speaks of THEE DAY of YAH, what it's referring to is THEE DAY of HIS return! …this is NOT going to be a very nice day!!! If you always thought that the day of YHWH (the LORD) was going to be a happy-happy day…on the following pages are just a few scriptures that 'graphically' describe the DAY of YAH!

Jeremiah 16:19

YHWH my strength, my fortress, my refuge in time of trouble (Day of Yah), the "gentiles" will
come to you from the ends of the earth, saying, "Our ancestors **inherited nothing but lies**,
futile idols, completely useless."

And so dear reader, it is up to each and every one of us to 'dig' and 'study' to find out what these lies are so we can **stop** believing the lie!

32 teach me what I have failed to see;
and if I have done wrong, I will do it no more'?
Job 34:32

DEAR READER, AGAIN, IT IS this writer's desire to encourage people to read the Scriptures for what they "actually" say and to not just believe what you have inherited or heard…

Shalom be with you always…**L.B.**

CIRCLE VERSES: THE DAY OF YAH

Amos 5:18 Woe to you who want the **Day of YHWH**! Why do you want it, this **Day of YAH**?

It is darkness, not light…

Isaiah 13:6 Howl! For **the Day of YHWH** is at hand, **destruction** coming from Shaddai.

Isaiah 63:1-6 Who is this, coming from Edom, from Botzrah with clothing stained crimson, so magnificently dressed, so stately in his great strength? "It is I, who speak victoriously, I well able to save." [2] Why is your apparel red, your clothes like someone treading a winepress? [3] "I have trodden the winepress alone; from the peoples, not one was with me. So I trod them in my anger, trampled them in **my fury**; so their lifeblood spurted out on my clothing, and I have stained all my garments; [4] for **the day of vengeance** that was in my heart and my year of redemption have come. [5] I looked, but there was no one to help, and I was appalled that no one upheld me. Therefore 'my own arm' brought me Y'shua (salvation), and **my own fury** upheld me. [6] In **my anger** I trod down the peoples, made them drunk with **my fury,** then poured out their lifeblood on the earth."

Jeremiah 46:10 [10] For on that **day YHWH** Elohei-Tzva'ot will have **a day of vengeance** for avenging himself on his enemies. The sword will **destroy**, have its fill, be made drunk on their **blood**. Yes, YHWH Elohei-Tzva'ot decrees **slaughter** in the land to the north by the Euphrates River.

Ezekiel 13:5 [5] You [prophets] have not gone up to the breaks in the barricade or repaired it for the house of Isra'el, so that they can stand fast in **battle** on the **day of YHWH**.

Joel 1:15 [15] "Oh no! The Day! **The Day of YHWH** is upon us! As **destruction** from Shaddai it is coming!

Joel 2:11 [11] YHWH shouts orders to his forces —**his army** is immense, mighty, and it does what he says. For great is the **Day of YHWH**, **fearsome, terrifying**! Who can endure it?

Joel 3:4 (2:31) The sun will be turned into **darkness** and the moon into **blood** before the coming of the great and **terrible Day of YHWH**."

Acts 2:20 [20] The sun will become **dark** and the moon **blood** before the great and **fearful Day of YHWH** comes.

Malachi 3:23 (4:5) [23] Look; I will send to you Eliyahu the prophet before the coming of the great and **terrible Day of YHWH**.

Zephaniah 1:14 [14] The great **Day of YHWH** is near, near and coming very quickly;
Hear the sound of the **Day of YHWH**! When it's here, even a warrior will **cry bitterly**.

1 Corinthians 5:5 [5] hand over such a person to the Adversary for his old nature to be **destroyed**, so that his spirit may be saved in the **Day of the YHWH**.

2 Peter 3:10 [10] However, the **Day of the YHWH** will come "like a thief." On that Day the **heavens will disappear** with a roar, the **elements will melt and disintegrate**, and the earth and everything in it **will be burned up**.

Revelation 14:14-20 [14] Then I looked, and there before me was a white cloud. Sitting on the cloud was someone like a Son of Man with a gold crown on his head and a **sharp sickle** in his hand. [15] Another angel came out of the Temple and shouted to the one sitting on the cloud, "Start using your sickle to reap, because the time to reap has come — the earth's harvest is ripe!" [16] The one sitting on the cloud swung his sickle over the earth, and **the earth was harvested.**
[17] Another angel came out of the Temple in heaven, and he too had **a sharp sickle**. [18] Then out from the altar went yet another angel, who was in charge of the **fire**; and he called in a loud voice to the one with the **sharp sickle**, "Use your **sharp sickle**, and gather the clusters of grapes from the earth's vine, because they are ripe!" [19] The angel swung his sickle down onto the earth, gathered the earth's grapes and threw them into the great winepress of **Elohim's fury**. [20] The winepress was trodden outside the city, and **blood flowed** from the winepress as high as the horses' bridles for two hundred miles!

Revelation 19:11-15 [11] Next I saw heaven opened, and there before me was a white horse. Sitting on it was the one called Faithful and True, and it is in righteousness that he passes judgment and **goes to battle**. [12] His eyes were like a fiery flame, and on his head were many royal crowns. And he had a name written which no one knew but himself. [13] He was wearing a robe that had been **soaked in blood**, and the name by which he is called is, "THE WORD OF GOD." [14] The **armies of heaven**, clothed in fine linen, white and pure, were following him on white horses. [15] And out of his mouth comes a **sharp sword** with which to strike down nations (gentiles) — "He will rule them with **a staff of iron."** It is he who treads the winepress from which flows the wine of the **furious rage of YHWH**, Elohim of **heaven's armies**.

Therefore Dear Reader

Stay alert,
Always praying that 'you' will be accounted worthy
To 'escape' all the things that will happen and to stand
in the presence of the
"Son of Man."
Luke 21:36

Shalom be with you always …**L.B.**

Revelation 10:3
Genesis 49:9
Hosea 11:10
Amos 1:2
Isaiah 31:4
Amos 3:4
Joel 4:16
Hosea 5:14

Lion Of The Tribe Of Y'hudah

Y'hudah (Judah; Jew)

YHWH LIKENS HIMSELF TO A **LION**, perhaps it's because all the characteristics of a **LION** are the same characteristics of YHWH. These characteristics are: Ruler; King; Devouring; Hunter; Leader; Mighty; Fearsome; Royal; Warrior; Majesty; Crown.

The verses in this circle speak to us about the 'imminent' intervention of YHWH in human affairs, speaks about how the tribe of Yahudah (Judah) will always be the 'Princely Tribe'-

Genesis 49:10

The scepter will not pass from **Y'hudah**, nor the ruler's staff from between his legs, until he comes to whom [obedience] belongs; and it is he (Messiah) whom the peoples will obey.

So it is NOT a coincidence the symbol of the banner of the Tribe of Yahudah is represented by a "**LION**" and that the Mashiach is of this tribe!

Genesis 49:9

⁹ Y'hudah is a **lion's** cub; <u>my son</u>, you stand over the prey.
He crouches down and stretches like a **lion**; like a lioness, who dares to provoke him

Numbers 2:2

² "The people of Isra'el are to set up camp by clans, each man with 'his own banner' and under his clan's **symbol**; they are to camp around the tent of meeting, but at a distance.

John 4:22

²² You people don't know what you are worshipping; we worship what we do know, because **Y'shua** (salvation) comes from **Yahudah** (the Jews).

This circle also speaks about how YHWH deals with the disobedient, Mashiachs' first coming was like unto a Lamb, but his second coming is as a **Lion**, he is coming to devour NOT to make peace but to 'separate' families, to 'kill' those who are contrary to YHWH.

Matthew 10:34-38

"Don't suppose that I have come to bring peace to the Land. It is not peace I have come to bring, but a **sword**! For I have come to set **a man against his father, a daughter against her mother, a daughter-in-law against her mother-in-law,** so that **a man's enemies will be the members of his own household.**
Whoever loves his father or mother more than he loves me is not worthy of me; anyone who loves his son or daughter more than he loves me is not worthy of me. And anyone who does not take up his execution-stake and follow me is not worthy of me.

Revelation speaks of this battle; our Messiah is 'literally' drenched in the blood of the rebellious!

Revelation 19:12-14

Next I saw heaven opened, and there before me was a white horse. Sitting on it was the one called Faithful and True, and it is in righteousness that he passes judgment and **goes to battle**. His eyes were like a **fiery flame**, and on his head were many **royal crowns**. And he had a name written which no one knew but himself. He was wearing a robe that had been **soaked in blood**, and the name by which he is called is, "THE WORD OF GOD." The armies of heaven, clothed in fine linen, white and pure, were following him on white horses.

(THE WAR MESSIAH)

Isaiah 59:17

[17] He put on righteousness as his **breastplate**,
salvation as a **helmet** on his head;
he clothed himself with garments of **vengeance**
and wrapped himself in **a mantle** of zeal.

"Dear Reader"

Stay alert, always praying that 'you' will be accounted worthy to 'escape' all these things that shall come to pass,
and to stand in the presence of the Son of Man.
Luke 21:36

CIRCLE VERSES: LION OF THE TRIBE OF Y'HUDAH

Hosea 5:14 [14] For to Efrayim I will be like a **lion**, and like a young lion to the house of Y'hudah —I will tear them up and go away; I will carry them off, and no one will rescue.

Hosea 11:10 [10] They will go after YHWH, who will **roar** like a **lion**; for he will **roar**, and the children will come trembling from the west.

Amos 1:2 [2] he said: YHWH is **roaring** from Tziyon thundering from Yerushalayim;
   the shepherds' pastures will mourn, and Mount Karmel's summit will wither.

Amos 3:4 [4] Does a **lion** roar in the forest when it has no prey? Does a young **lion** growl in his lair if it has caught nothing?

Joel 4:16 [16] YHWH will **roar** from Tziyon, he will thunder from Yerushalayim, the sky and the earth will shake. But YHWH will be a refuge for "his" people, a stronghold for the people of Isra'el.

Isaiah 31:4 [4] For here is what YHWH says to me: "As a **lion or lion cub** growls at its prey and isn't frightened away by the shouts of hordes of shepherds called out against him — their voices do not upset him — so likewise YHWH-Tzva'ot will descend **to fight** on Mount Tziyon, on its hill.

Genesis 49:9 [9] Y'hudah is a **lion's** cub; my son, you stand over the prey.
   He crouches down and stretches like a **lion**; like a **lioness**, who dares to provoke him?

Revelation 10:3 [3] and shouted in a voice as loud as the **roar of a lion**; and when he shouted, seven thunderclaps sounded with voices that spoke.

May YAH make his face to shine upon you and give you Shalom (completeness)…**L.B.**

PSALM 118:19

Open the gates of righteousness for me;

I will enter them and thank Yah.

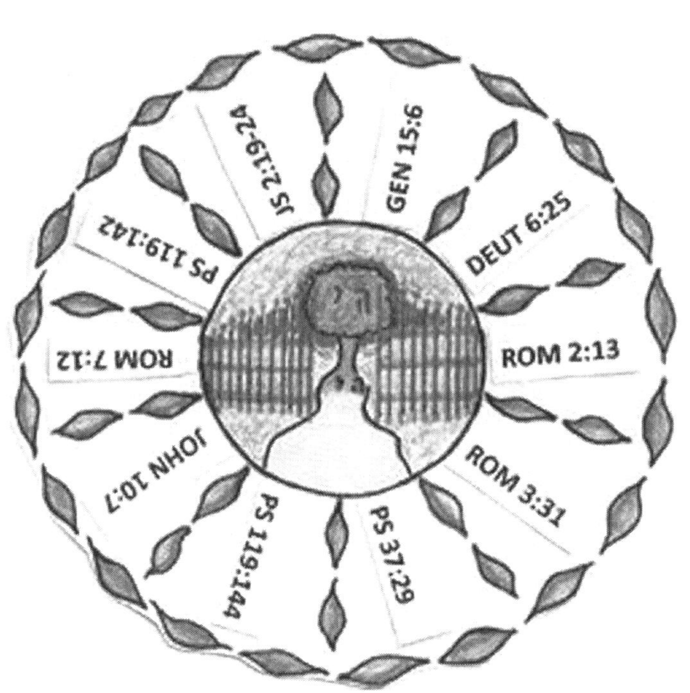

Righteousness

Biblical righteousness is NOT what we have been taught, so let's see how YHWH defines righteousness:

Psalm 119:144
Your **Torah** (instruction) is **righteous'** forever'; give me understanding, and I will live.

Psalm 119:142
Your **righteousness is eternal righteousness**, and your "*Torah* is truth".

Psalm 119:160
The main thing about your word (Torah) is that it's true; and all your **righteous** rulings last forever.

Psalm 119:165
[165] Those who **love your *Torah*** have great Shalom (completeness); nothing makes them stumble.

So we see that **Torah** is **Righteous** and **True** and is **FOREVER !** Now let's see what the brother of Mashiach (Messiah) said about 'righteousness':

James 2:22-24
[22] You see that his faith worked **with** his actions; by the 'actions' the faith was made 'complete'; [23] and the passage of the *Torah was* fulfilled which says, "Abraham had faith in Elohim, and it was credited to his account as **righteousness**." He was even called Elohim's friend. [24] You see that a person is declared **righteous** because of actions and NOT because of faith alone.

Obviously those "actions" must be 'everything' YHWH commanded us through Mosheh and NOT our own ideas such as: the calf incident in the wilderness (Exo 32:1-4); Xmas (Jer 10:2) or Ishtar/Easter (Jer 7:18; Lev 20:1-5; Dt 18:10; 2Kg 16:3; 17:17; 21:6; 23:10; Eze 20:31; 2Chron 33:6) and many more! Faith is "DOING" what he told us to do without questioning it…just like Abraham did with Isaac.

<u>**Romans 2:13**</u>
For it is not merely the 'hearers' of *Torah* whom Elohim considers righteous; rather, **it is the 'doers' of what *Torah* says who will be made righteous in Elohim's sight**

Stray from his Torah and you become unrighteous…pretty self explanatory!

CIRCLE VERSES: Righteousness

James 2:19-24 You believe that "Elohim is one"? Good for you! The demons believe it too — the thought makes them shudder with fear! [20] But, foolish fellow, do you want to be shown that such "faith" apart from actions is barren? [21] Wasn't *Abraham avinu* declared **righteous** because of actions when he offered up his son Yitz'chak on the altar? [22] You see that his faith worked with his actions; by the actions the faith was made complete; [23] and the passage of the Torah was fulfilled which says, "Abraham had faith in God, and it was credited to his account as **righteousness**." He was even called Elohim's friend. [24] You see that a person is declared **righteous** because of actions and NOT because of faith alone.

Psalm 119:142 Your **righteousness** is eternal **righteousness,** and your *Torah* is truth.

Psalm 119:144 Your instruction **(Torah) is righteous** forever; give me understanding, and I will live.

Psalm 37:29 The **righteous** will inherit the land and live in it forever**.**

Romans 2:13 For it is not merely the hearers of *Torah* whom Elohim considers **righteous**; rather, it is the 'doers' of what *Torah* says who will be made **righteous** in Elohim's sight.

Romans 3:31 Does it follow that we abolish *Torah* by this trusting (faith)? Heaven forbid! On the contrary, **we confirm Torah**.

Romans 7:12 So **the *Torah* is holy**; that is, the commandment is **holy, just and good**.

Deuteronomy 6:25 It will be **righteousness** for us 'IF' we are careful to obey all these *mitzvot* (commandments) before YHWH our Elohim, just as he ordered us to do.'"

Genesis 15:6 He believed in *YHWH*, and he credited it to him as **righteousness**.

John 10:7 So Y'shua said to them again, "Yes, indeed!" I tell you that I am the gate for the sheep (**righteous**).

REMEMBER THE DAY SHABBAT, TO SET IT APART FOR YHWH!

EXODUS 20:8

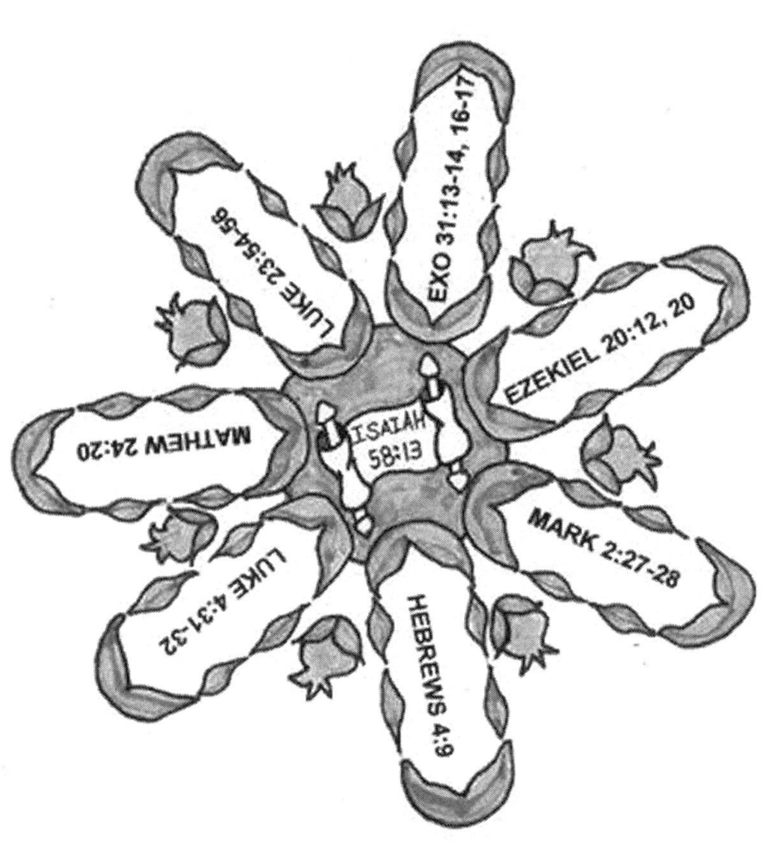

SHABBAT (SABBATH)

HAVE YOU EVER BEEN TOLD you don't have to keep the Sabbath because that was for "those" people or we keep Sunday because Messiah rose on Sunday, well let's see what YHWH says!

Exodus 31:17

The people of Isra'el are to keep the Shabbat, to observe Shabbat through all their generations as 'a perpetual covenant'.
It (Sabbath) is a sign between me and the children of Isra'el foooreverrr!!!; for in six days YHWH made heaven and earth, but on the 'seventh' day he stopped working and rested."

So ask yourself… How long is forever???

Hebrews 4:9

So there remains a Shabbat-keeping for Elohim's (Gods) people.

So ask yourself… are YOU one of Elohim's people???

Matthew 5:18

Yes indeed! I tell you that 'until heaven and earth pass away', not so much as a yud or a stroke will pass from the Torah — not until everything that must happen has happened.

So ask yourself… are Heaven and Earth still here???

Never ever anywhere in scripture does YHWH tell us to keep any other day of the week "Holy"- NEVER! He tells us over and over and over again to "REMEMBER" and "GUARD" and "KEEP" the "SABBATH", this is a command NOT a suggestion!

He says over and over -these are MY Sabbaths, these are MY Holy Days, these are MY Feasts. He NEVER said, the Sabbath is for Y'hudah (Jews) only or these are the Feasts of the Jews, he NEVER said the SABBATH is a sign between ME and Y'hudah (Jews)…NO! He said it is a sign between ME and the "CHILDREN OF ISRAEL"!!! FooorEverrr!!!

Dear reader, please don't let ANYONE ever tell you that you don't have to do "those" things anymore because they have been done away with, because that is the greatest LIE ever told by the FATHER of ALL LIES!!!

Daniel 7:25

He (Anti-Messiah) will speak words against the Most High and try to exhaust the holy ones of
the Most High.
He will think to **change** the seasons (moedim, appointed times of YAH) and the law (Torah);

Psalm 119:33

Teach me, *YHWH*, the way of YOUR laws;
KEEPING them will be its own 'reward' for me.

Job 34:32

Teach me what I have failed to see;
and if I have done wrong, I will do it no more'!

You're probably asking yourself; can't we worship him on any day? Does it really matter what day it is? Answer: Yes and Yes! In fact we should worship him every day! But you MUST worship him on the **SHABBAT** this is a command NOT a suggestion! In fact it is the longest and most detailed of all the Ten Commandments!

How does YHWH punish the disobedient? The same way he always has, just like our first parents were punished: EXILE; SCATTER (GET OUT FROM BEFORE MY FACE!)

Jeremiah 15:1

Then YHWH said to me, "Even if Moshe and Sh'mu'el were standing in front of me, my heart
would not turn toward this people! **Drive them out of my sight, get them out of here**!

YHWH goes on and on about why he EXILED (punished) Y'srael by scattering us among the Heathen (Gentiles/Nations). He figured- You want to behave like a heathen, then go and be one! This is our punishment.

Ezekiel 20:23-24

[23] "I also raised my hand and swore to them in the desert that I would **scatter them among the gentiles** and disperse them through the countries; [24] because they hadn't obeyed my rulings but had rejected my laws and profaned **MY *Shabbats***, and their eyes had turned toward their fathers' idols.

Isaiah 66:23

[23] "Every month on Rosh-Hodesh and every week on **Shabbat**,
everyone living will come
to worship in my presence," says YHWH.

Ezekiel 20:12-13

[12] I gave them **MY *Shabbats*** as a sign between me and them, so that they would know that I, *YHWH*, am the one who makes them kadosh (holy).
[13] "'But the house of Isra'el rebelled against me in the desert. They did not live by MY laws; and they rejected MY rulings, which, if a person does, he will have life through them; moreover, they greatly profaned **MY *Shabbats***. Then I said I would pour out my fury on them in the desert, in order to destroy them.

Ezekiel 20:15-16

[15] Yet I also raised my hand and swore to them in the desert that I would not bring them into the land I was giving them, a land flowing with milk and honey, the most beautiful of all lands; [16] because they had rejected MY rulings, did not live by MY laws and profaned **MY *Shabbats***; since their hearts went after their idols.

Ezekiel 20:21

[21] "'But the children rebelled against me. They did not live by MY laws or observe MY rulings, to obey them, which, if a person does, he will have life by them; and they profaned **MY *Shabbats***. Then I said I would pour out my fury on them and spend my anger on them in the desert.

Ezekiel 22:8

[8] You treat my holy things with contempt, you profane **MY *Shabbats***.

Ezekiel 22:26

[26] Her *cohanim* have done violence to my *Torah*, profaned my holy things, made no difference between the holy and the common, not distinguished between unclean and clean, hidden their eyes from **MY *Shabbats***, and profaned me among themselves.

Ezekiel 23:38

Moreover, they have done this to me as well: they defiled my sanctuary on the same day, and they profaned **MY *Shabbats***.

So ask yourself, 'whose' Sabbath are you keeping???

SHABBAT SHALOM!

I have found 'At least' 255 quotes from cover to cover referring to the 7th day, and when YAH says something well over 200 times, I think we better pay close attention don't you?

172 'SHABBAT/SABBATH ' Quotes:

Genesis (1)
1 Esdras (2)
Exodus (16)
Leviticus (17)
Numbers (3)
Deuteronomy (3)
2 Kings (5)
Isaiah (6)
Jeremiah (5)
Ezekiel (15)
Hosea (1)
Amos (1)
Psalm (1)
Lamentations (1)
Nehemiah (10)

1 Chronicles (2)
2 Chronicles (6)
Matthew (9)
Mark (10)
Luke (17)
John (10)
Acts (9)
1 Corinthians (1)
Colossians (1)
Hebrews (1)
Judith (2)
1 Esdras (2)
1 Maccabees (10)
2 Maccabees (7)

83 'Seventh Day' Quotes

Genesis (4)
Exodus (15)
Leviticus (18)
Numbers (11)
Deuteronomy (2)
Joshua (2)
Judges (2)
2 Samuel (1)
1 Kings (2)

Greek Ester (1)
2 Kings (2)
2 Chronicles (1)
Ezra (1)
Nehemiah (2)
Tobit (1)
Esther (1)
2 Maccabees (3)
3 Maccabees (1)

Jeremiah (1)
Baruch (1)
Ezekiel (5)
Daniel (1)
Haggai (1)
Hebrews (1)
Revelation (1)
2 Esdras (2)

For a grand total of 255!

On the following pages you will find out why you or someone you know worships and keeps Sunday instead of the day YHWH commands us to keep.

Those who have ears,
Let 'them' hear what the ru'ach (spirit) is saying…
Revelation 2:7, 11, 17, 29; 3:6, 13, 22; 13:9
Mathew 13:9; **Mark** 4:23; **Luke** 14:35

Who changed the Sabbath of YAH, more importantly who gave it the power to do so?

Council of Laodicea

At the Council of Laodicea in 364 C.E. the following crimes against YHWH were decreed:

"Christians" shall not Judaize and be idle on **Saturday**, the **Sabbath**, but shall work on THAT day; but the Lord's day (Sunday) they shall honor, and as being Christians, shall if possible, do no work on that day. If, however, they are found **Judaizing**, they shall be shut off from Christ."

This, my dear reader is an abomination and sin against YHWH, firstly being loyal to YHWH is NOT Judaizing, it is YHWHaizing! The SHABBAT was NOT made only for Y'hudah (Jews), it was made for mankind…ALL of us! There weren't any Hebrews, Israelites and much less Jews when YHWH created and blessed and sanctified the SHABBAT in Genesis 2:3.

Daniel 7:25

He (Anti-Messiah) will speak words against the Most High and try to exhaust the holy ones of the Most High. He will think to CHANGE the appointed times (Feasts of YHWH) and the law (Torah).

So now we know from whom it gets its power to CHANGE YHWH's times, from the Anti-Messiah himself! The book of Revelation speaks of this "Laodicea":

Revelation 3:14-22

[14] "To the angel of the congregation in **Laodicea**, write: 'Here is the message from the *Amein*, the faithful and true witness, the Ruler of Elohim's creation: [15] "I know what you are doing: you are neither cold nor hot. How I wish you were either one or the other! [16] So, because you are lukewarm, neither cold nor hot, **I will vomit you out of my mouth!** [17] For you keep saying, 'I am rich, I have gotten rich, I don't need a thing!' You don't know that you are the one who is wretched, pitiable, poor, blind and naked! [18] My advice to you is to buy from me gold refined by fire, so that you may be rich; and white clothing, so that you may be dressed and not have to be **ashamed of your nakedness**; and eye salve to rub on your eyes, so that you may see. [19] As for me, I rebuke and discipline everyone I love; so exert yourselves, and **turn from your sins!** [20] Here, I'm standing at the door, knocking. If someone hears my voice and opens the door, I will come in to him and eat with him, and he will eat with me. [21] I will let him who wins the victory sit with me on my throne, just as I myself also won the victory and sat down with my Father on his throne. [22] Those who have ears, let them hear what the Spirit is saying to the congregations.'"

So now we see that the Holy **Sabbath day** of YHWH was CHANGED by a Pagan Roman Emperor who received his power from none other than the Anti-Messiah himself!

Therefore if you are keeping Sunday, you are actually obeying a pagan Roman Emperor, the Pope's of Rome and worshipping the Anti-Messiah instead of our Creator. You are therefore Anti-YHWH!

Does this shock you? If it does shock you- then I assume you never heard about the **SHABBAT**, and if you never heard about the **SHABBAT** then you must not have read the Bible and if you never read the Bible can you then claim "ignorance" on THAT DAY?

Acts 17:30

"In the past", YHWH overlooked such **ignorance**; **but now** he is commanding ALL people everywhere to turn (T'shuvah) to him from their sins.

Back in the day the common people did NOT have access to the Scriptures like you and I do today, most couldn't even read, however, in these days you and I live in, we have an abundance of knowledge at our fingertips!

Daniel 12:4

But thou, O Daniel, shut up the words, and seal the book, even to the time of the end: many shall run to and fro, and **knowledge (Torah) shall be increased**.

He is NOT speaking of worldly knowledge; he is speaking of YHWH knowledge. We, living today will have NO excuse; we will NOT be able to play the "Ignorance" card! Unless of course you are deaf, blind and have never been taught to read 'Braille', or are severely mentally incapacitated.

On the following pages you will see just how arrogant the Anti-Messiah is, he is so full of himself that he openly admits there is NO biblical authority to observing Sunday and throwing away YHWH's **Shabbat!** They ADMITT IT!!!

Roman Catholic "AND" Protestant Confessions about Sunday

<u>T. Enright, C.S.S.R., in a lecture at Hartford, Kansas, Feb. 18,**1884**.</u>

"I have repeatedly offered $1,000 to anyone who can prove to me from the Bible alone that I am bound to keep Sunday holy. There is no such law in the Bible. It is a law of the holy Catholic Church alone. **The Bible says, 'Remember the Sabbath day to keep it holy.'** **The Catholic Church says: NO!** By **MY** 'divine' power **I abolish the Sabbath day** and command you to keep holy the first day of the week.' And lo! The entire civilized world bows down in a reverent obedience to the command of the holy Catholic Church."

<u>Peter Geiermann, C.S.S.R., The Converts Catechism of Catholic Doctrine (**1957**), p. 50.</u>

<u>"Question:</u> Which is the **Sabbath** day?

<u>"Answer:</u> **Saturday** is the **Sabbath** day.

<u>"Question:</u> Why do we observe Sunday instead of **Saturday**?

<u>"Answer:</u> We observe Sunday instead of **Saturday** because **the Catholic Church** transferred the solemnity from **Saturday** to Sunday."

<u>Peter R. Kraemer, Catholic Church Extension Society (**1975**), Chicago, Illinois.</u>

"Regarding the change from the observance of the Jewish **Sabbath** to the Christian Sunday, I wish to draw your attention to the facts: (F.Y.I. It is NOT the Jewish Sabbath, it is YHWH's Sabbath: My emphasis.)

"1) That Protestants, who accept the Bible as the only rule of faith and religion, should by all means go back to the observance of the **Sabbath**. The fact that they do not, but on the contrary observe the Sunday, stultifies them in the eyes of every thinking man.

"2) **We Catholics do not accept the Bible as the only rule of faith**. Besides the Bible we have the living Church, the authority of the Church, as a rule to guide us. We say, this Church, instituted by Christ to teach and guide man through life, has the right to change the ceremonial laws of the Old Testament and hence, we accept her change of the **Sabbath** to Sunday. We frankly say, yes, **the Church made this change**, made this law, as she made many other laws, for instance, the Friday abstinence, the unmarried priesthood, the laws concerning mixed marriages, the regulation of Catholic marriages and a thousand other laws. **"It is always somewhat laughable; to see the Protestant churches, in pulpit and legislation, demand the observance of Sunday, of which there is nothing in their Bible."**

Baptist Dr. Edward T. Hiscox, a paper read before a New York ministers' conference, Nov. 13, **1893**, reported in New York Examiner, Nov.16, **1893**.

"**There was and is a commandment to keep holy the Sabbath day**, but that **Sabbath** day was not Sunday. It will be said, however, and with some show of triumph, that the **Sabbath** was transferred from the seventh to the first day of the week …. Where can the record of such a transaction be found? Not in the New Testament **absolutely not.**

"To me it seems unaccountable that Jesus, during three years' intercourse with His disciples, often conversing with them upon the **Sabbath** question . . . **never** alluded to any transference of the day; also, that during forty days of His resurrection life, no such thing was intimated.

"Of course, I quite well know that Sunday did come into use in early Christian history . . . . But what a pity it comes branded with the mark of paganism, and christened with the name of the sun god, adopted and sanctioned by the papal apostasy, and bequeathed as a sacred legacy to Protestantism!"

Alexander Campbell, The Christian Baptist, Feb. 2, **1824**, vol. 1. no. 7, p. 164.

'But', say some, it was changed from the seventh to the first day.' Where? when? And by whom? No man can tell. No; **it never was changed, nor could it be**, unless creation was to be gone through again: for the reason assigned must be changed before the observance, or respect to the reason, can be changed! It is all old wives' fables to talk of the change of the **Sabbath** from the seventh to the first day. **If it be changed, it was that august personage changed it who changes times and laws ex officio - I think his name is Doctor Antichrist.'**

Dear, dear reader, these confessions go on and on and on, they are very easily googled, like I said earlier, we have 'abundant' knowledge at our fingertips! Daniel's prophecy is being fulfilled…Knowledge HAS increased! The "ignorance" card is no longer an option!

As Mr. T. Enright said in a lecture at Hartford, Kansas, Feb. 18,**1884**:

"The entire civilized world bows down in a reverent obedience to the command of the holy Catholic Church." ! (The Popes)

Dear, dear reader, it's time to wake up!

<u>HE DECEIVES THE WHOLE WORLD!!!</u>

<u>Revelation 12:9</u>
The great Dragon, that ancient serpent, called the Devil and Satan, which **deceives the whole world:** he was cast out into the earth and his angels were cast down with him.

<u>Isaiah 42:8</u>
"I am YHWH: that is my name: and **my glory will I not give to another**, neither my praise to graven images."

<u>Isaiah 66:23</u>
Every month and every week on **SHABBAT**, everyone living will come to worship in my presence says YHWH

<u>Mathew 12:8</u>
"The Son of Man is Master of the **SABBATH**"

The weekly **Sabbath** of Israel was not only a sign of the covenant between Elohim and them, but also a witness to all the nations/gentiles that **Israel was a special people set apart** from others to receive the revelation of Elohim (God), and to bring the Messiah into the world.

<u>Sh'mot (Deut) 31:13-14</u>
"Speak thou also unto the children of Israel, saying, verily **MY Sabbaths** ye shall keep: for it is a sign between me and you throughout your generations; that ye may know that I am YHVH that doth sanctify you. Ye shall keep the **Sabbath** therefore; for it is holy unto you: **every one that defiles it shall surely be put to death**: for <u>whosoever</u> doeth any work therein, that soul shall be cut off from among his people."

<u>Revelation 2:23</u>
23 And **I** will kill her children (those that follow her doctrine) with a death. And all the congregations will know that **I** am the One searching minds and hearts, and **I** will give to you, to each one, according to your works.

<u>Revelation 18:4</u>
And I heard another voice from heaven, saying, **Come out of her, my people**, that ye be not partakers of her sins, and that ye receive not of her plagues.

<u>John 8:32</u>
32 And ye shall know the truth (Torah), and the truth (Torah) shall make you free.

CIRCLE VERSES: Sʜᴀʙʙᴀᴛ

LUKE 4:31-32 He went down to K'far-Nachum, a town in the Galil, on **SHABBAT** as was his custom. They were amazed at the way he taught, because his word carried the ring of authority.

Luke 23:54-56 It was Preparation Day, and a **SHABBAT** was about to begin. The women who had come with Yahshua from the Galil followed; they saw the tomb and how his body was placed in it. Then they went back home to prepare spices and ointments. On **SHABBAT** the women rested, in obedience to the commandment.

Mark 2:27-28 Then he said to them, "**SHABBAT** "was made for mankind, not mankind for **SHABBAT** "; so the son of man is Master even of the **SHABBAT**".

Mathew 24:20 Pray that you will not have to escape in winter or on the **SHABBAT**.

Ezekiel 20:12, 20 I gave them **MY SHABBATS** as a sign between me and them, so that they would know that I, YHWH, am the one who makes them Holy. And keep **MY SHABBATS** Holy; and they will be a sign between me and you, so that you will know that I am YHWH your Elohim.

Exodus 31:13-14, 16-17 "Tell the children of Israel". You are to observe **MY SHABBATS** for this is a sign between me and you throughout all your generations; so that you will know that I am YHWH, who sets you apart for me. Therefore you are to keep **MY SHABBAT**, because it is set apart for you. Everyone who treats it as ordinary must be put to death; for whoever does any work on it is to be cut off from his people. The people of Israel are to keep the **SHABBAT**, to observe **SHABBAT** through ALL their generations **as a perpetual covenant**. It is a sign between me and the people of Israel FOOOREVERRR !!!; for in six days YHWH made heaven and earth, but on the **SEVENTH** day he stopped working and rested."

Isaiah 58:13-14 [13] *"If you hold back your foot on **Shabbat** from pursuing your own interests on **my holy day**; if you call **Shabbat** a delight, **YHWH's holy day**, "worth honoring"; then honor it <u>by not doing 'your' usual things or pursuing 'your' interests or speaking about them</u>.* [14] ***'If'** you do, you will find delight in YHWH — I will make you ride on the heights of the land and feed you with the heritage of your ancestor Ya'akov (Yisra'el), for the mouth of YHWH has spoken."*

Dear Reader, there are '10' commandments NOT '9', it is the one commandment the whole world seems to hate, because the Devil deceives the Whole World!

<u>Hebrews 4:9</u>
So there remains a **SHABBAT-keeping** for "YHWH's people".
hallelu**YAH...L.B**

Ha Shem

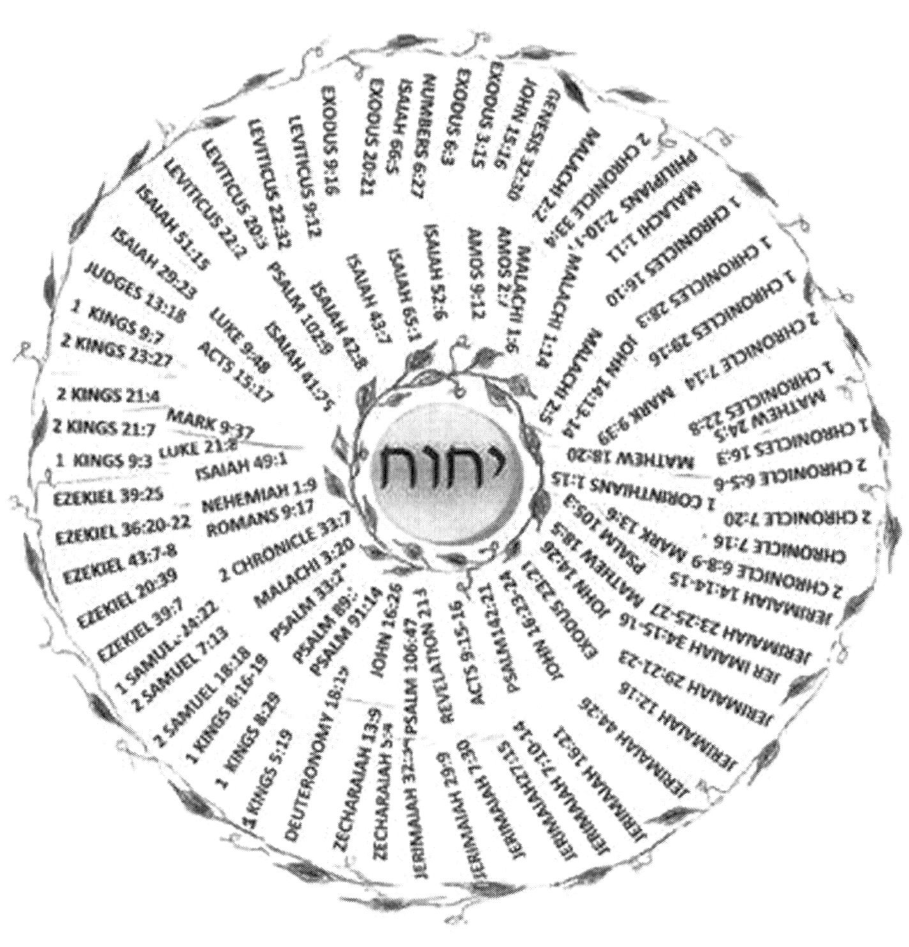

The Shabbat isn't the only thing the anti-messiah changed, he also changed Elohims' Shem (name), and he also caused Y'srael to 'forget' Elohims' name! YHWH tells us through his neviim (prophets), the following…

Jeremiah 23:27
With their dreams that they keep telling each other, they hope to **cause my people to forget my name**; just as their ancestors **forgot** **my name** when they worshipped Ba'al.

Ezekiel 36:21
But I am concerned about **my holy name**, which the house of Isra'el is "profaning" among the goyim (gentiles, nations) where they have gone.

Proverbs 30:4
Who has gone up to heaven and come down? Who has cupped the wind in the palms of his hands? Who has wrapped up the waters in his cloak? Who established all the ends of the earth? What is **his name,** and what is **his son's name?** Surely you know!

Most people do NOT use our creator's name, they simply call him God; Lord; The Almighty; Father; Adonai and Ha Shem- these are NOT his name these are titles. Except for Ha Shem, this is what observant "Jews" call him. How can anyone want to call the Creator of Heaven and Earth…the name??!! How can you bless his name by saying…'I bless the name the name'??!!! This is ridiculous!!

Elohim wants us to call him by **his NAME**, he wants us to Bless **his NAME**, he wants us to make **his NAME** known throughout the Earth, consider the following…

Exodus 9:16
But it is for this very reason that I have kept you alive — to show you my power, and so that **my NAME may 'resound' throughout the whole earth.**

Exodus 3:15

Elohim said to Mosheh, "Say this to the people of Isra'el:**'YHWH'** the Elohim of your fathers, the Elohim of Avraham, the Elohim of Yitz'chak and the Elohim of Ya'akov, has sent me to you.' **This is my NAME <u>foooreverrr!</u>**; this is how I am to be remembered generation after generation.

Acts 9:15

[15] But YHWH said to him, "Go, because this man is my chosen instrument **to carry my name to the *Goyim/Gentiles,***

even to their kings, and to the sons of Isra'el as well.

Isaiah 42:8

"I am **YHWH**: that is **my NAME**:. . .

Exodus 20:7

[7] Thou shalt not take the **NAME of YHWH** thy Elohim in vain (shaw); for   YHWH will not hold him guiltless that taketh his **name** in shaw (vain).

The hebrew word used in the Third Commandment for "vain" is shin-vav-alef - pronounced " shaw " and means: worthlessness; false; empty. Literally understood as - do NOT call me by a "FALSE " name! This does NOT mean: Do not use my name, on the contrary, he wants us to use his PROPER name NOT a false one.

Jeremiah 16:19

[19]..."Our ancestors inherited nothing but lies, futile idols, completely useless."

Not only did HaSatan change Yah's name, he also changed his sons' name!

There NEVER existed a Biblical person named 'Jesus'. Jesus is NOT a translation because a translation of a word equals the definition of the word being translated. Therefore the proper translation of Y'shua is saviour/salvation, The sons'name literally means: 'YAH' SAVES! Because the NAME of the FATHER is in the NAME of the SON!

Nor is 'Jesus' a transliteration, a 'Transliteration' is simply phonetically sounding-out a word of one language with the letters/alphabet of different language, causing the pronunciation to sound "identical" to the word being transliterated and 'Jesus' 'sounds' nothing like 'y'shua".

The letter "J" did NOT exist in ANY language until about 450 years ago! And there still is NOT a "J" sound in the Hebrew language. The name 'Jesus' is actually a 'transliteration' of the Greek name "IESOUS", except for the newly invented "J" it is the exact pronunciation/sound: YESOUS- JESUS, actually the ending is "SOUS "or "ZEUS" in the English. Could it be? Could the ancient Greeks have applied the name of their false deity "ZEUS" to the son of Elohim because of their "mixing" paganism with truth? Hmmm… Dear reader please **STOP** reading now and flip to the glossary and look-up the word " iesous ", then return and consider the following…

John 5:43

[43] I have come in my Father's name, and you do NOT receive me; if '<u>another</u>' comes <u>in his own name</u>, "him" you will receive.

<u>Romans 10:13</u>

[13] since *everyone* who calls on the **NAME** of **YHWH** will be delivered.

<u>Acts 4:12</u>

[12] There is Yahshua (salvation) in no one else! For **there is no other NAME** under heaven given to mankind by whom we must be saved!"

<u>Acts 10:43</u>

[43] ALL the prophets bear witness to him, that everyone who puts his trust in him receives forgiveness of sins **through his NAME**."

<u>Matthew 21:9</u>

The crowds ahead of him and behind shouted, "Please! Deliver us!" to the Son of David; "Blessed is he who comes **in the NAME of *YHWH* !"** "You in the highest heaven! Please! Deliver us!"

<u>Philippians 2:10</u>

[10] that in honor of **the name** given **Y'shua**, every knee will bow — in heaven, on earth and under the earth —

'We wouldn't apply the Egyptian god names - Ra or Osiris to YHWH. So why would you apply the Greek god name -Zeus to our Messiah?'

It isn't ONLY about using his 'literal' name; it is much deeper than that. Knowing and using his name encompasses his "character" and "ALL" that he stands for…his very 'essence'! Consider the following…

<u>Leviticus 20:3</u>

I too will set myself against him and cut him off from his people, because he has **sacrificed his child to Molekh**, defiling my sanctuary and 'profaning' **my HOLY NAME**.

<u>Amos 2:7</u>

Grinding the heads of the poor in the dust and pushing the lowly out of the way; father and son sleep with the same girl, 'profaning' **my HOLY NAME**;

As we see in the above verses, we understand that our "actions" also - either Honour or Defile YHWH's name/character, the above verses aren't about 'verbally' uttering his name, they are about literally "DOING" what he told us NOT to do in his Torah (instruction) he gave us through his eved (servant) Mosheh, therefore **defiling his name**. Consider the following verse…

<u>1 Timothy 6:1</u>

6 Those who are under the yoke of slavery(service) should regard their masters as worthy of full respect, so that the **NAME** of Elohim AND the teaching (TORAH) will not be brought into disrepute.

The above verse 1Timothy 6:1 is a beautiful analogy of our relationship with Yah, we are his evedim (servants/ slaves), remember the Hebrew word "eved" is the same word for slave or servant and Yah is our Master! Compare with the following…

Leviticus 25:55
55 For to me the people of Isra'el are slaves (evedeem); they are my slaves whom I brought out of the land of Egypt; I am *YHWH* your Elohim.

I, for one am honoured to be Yah's eved! And an eved does ALL his/her Master requests.

Ezekiel 39:7
7 I will make my holy name known among **my** people Isra'el; I will not allow **my holy name** to be profaned any longer. Then the *Goyim/Gentiles* will know that I am *YHWH*,
the Holy One of Isra'el.

Isaiah 52:5-6
5 So now, what should I do here," asks *YHWH*,"since my people were carried off for nothing? Their oppressors are howling," says *YHWH*, "and **my name** is insulted, daily.
6 Therefore my people will know my name; therefore on that day they will know
that I, the one speaking — here I am!"

Psalm 91:14
14 "Because he loves me, I will rescue him;
because he **knows my name,** I will protect him.

So now we understand that when the anti-messiah changed Yah's name; character; moedim (festivals of Yah) and his Torah (law) this changed his entire "**IMAGE**". The "**IMAGE**" being put forth by Xtianity was fabricated by the Pagan Roman Church, their depiction of the Messiah is an…Anti-YHWH, Anti-semetic, Covenant-breaking, Pork-eating, Effeminate-looking J.C. dude! This my dear reader is NOT the "I**MAGE**" of our Mashiach (Messiah) who "is" YHWH in the flesh!!!!! This my dear reader is the "**IMAGE**" of the Anti-Messiah! Consider the following…

Hebrews 1:3
3 This Son is the radiance of the Sh'khinah, the very expression (**exact" image"**) of Elohim's essence, upholding ALL that exists by his powerful word (Torah); and after he had, through himself, made purification for sins, he sat down at the right hand of
Ha G'dulah Ba M'romim. (the greatness/majesty on high).

John 10:30

I and the Father are **echad** (one /inseparable).

Isaiah 45:21
…Wasn't it I, **YHWH** ? There is **no other** Elohim besides me, a just <u>Elohim</u> **'AND'** <u>a Savior</u>;
there is <u>none</u> besides me.
(YHWH is Messiah and Messiah is YHWH)
Isa 45:15; 49:29; 60:16; Hos 13:4; Zeph 3:17;
Ps 27:9; 43:5; Luke 14:7; Acts 5:31 and many more.

Matthew 24:24; Mark 13:22
For there will appear **false Messiahs** and **false** <u>prophets performing</u> great miracles — amazing
things! — so as to fool even the chosen, if possible.

Matthew 7:22-23
[22] On that Day, 'many ' will say to me, 'L-rd, L-rd! Didn't we prophesy **in your name**? Didn't we
expel demons **in your name**? Didn't we perform many miracles **in your name**?' [23] Then I will
tell them to their faces, 'I never knew you! **Get away from me, you workers of lawlessness
(TorahLESSness) !**

1 Timothy 6:3-4
[3]If <u>anyone</u> teaches **a different doctrine** and does not agree to the sound precepts of our
Master Yashua the Messiah AND to the doctrine that is **in keeping with godliness (YHWH/
Torah)**, he is puffed up with conceit knowing NOTHING….!!!!!

Galatians 1:6-7
[6] I am astounded that you are so quick to remove yourselves from me, the one who called you
by the Messiah's grace, and turn to **some 'other' supposedly "Good News,"**[7] which is not
good news at all! What is really happening is that certain people are trying to **pervert the
"genuine" Good News of the Messiah.**

Could this false "**IMAGE**" created by Satan through the Roman Catholic Church and accepted by the 'so-called' protesting churches be the "**IMAGE**" spoken of in Revelation? Consider the following. . .

Revelation 14:9-10
[9] Another angel, a third one, followed them and said in a loud voice, "If anyone worships the beast and "**its IMAGE**" and receives the mark on his forehead (our acceptance) or on his hand (our praise), [10] he will indeed drink the wine of Elohim's fury poured undiluted into the cup of his rage. He will be tormented by fire and sulfur before the holy angels and before the Lamb,

Dear reader, this 'fabricated' false "**IMAGE**" of Messiah being preached by Christians today does NOT match the description given by **YHWH** himself ! Here is what **YHWH** said about Y'shua…

Deuteronomy 18:18-19
I will raise up for them a prophet like you(Mosheh) from among their kinsmen. **I will put MY words in his mouth, and he will tell them everything I order him.** Whoever doesn't listen to **MY words**, which **he will speak in MY NAME**, will have to account for himself to me.
(Word = Torah)

Exodus 23:21
[21] Pay attention to him, listen to what he says and do not rebel against him; because he will not forgive any wrongdoing of yours, since **MY NAME (essence) resides "in" him.**
(YAH/YAHSHUA)

And so if the fathers' NAME resides in the sons' NAME…Then how can his sons 'NAME be Jeezeus???

And if YHWH said Messiah would ONLY speak the SAME words of YHWH then why do Christians teach that YHWH's word (Torah) was done away with and now we have Christ's New Law??? This is Biblically IMPOSSIBLE and is an ABOMINATION and AFFRONT to my KING YHWH!!!!! New Law??!!

Isaiah 64:4
[4 (5)] You favored those who were glad to do justice, those who remembered you in <u>your ways</u>. When you were angry, we kept sinning; but " if" we keep your "**ancient**" ways, we will be saved.

Proverbs 28:4 (Biblical definition of 'Wicked')
[4] Those who "abandon" *Torah* praise the wicked, but those who "keep" *Torah* fight them.

So much for Christs' "new law"!! (Ecc 1:9…NOTHING NEW under the sun!!) Therefore we MUST worship him and honour him in Truth and this Truth obviously includes his TRUE NAME, his TRUE IMAGE, his TRUE GOSPEL and the TRUTH will make us free. Free of what? Free of the LIES!

And so dear reader, worship him in TRUTH (Torah), Glorify the NAME YHWH!

Alechaim and Shalom be with you always…**L.B.**

CIRCLE VERSES: HaShem (The Name)

Genesis 32:30 Ya'akov(Jacob/Israel) asked him, "Please tell me **your name**." But he answered, "Why are you asking about **MY NAME**?" and blessed him there.

Exodus 3:15 Elohim said further to Moshe, "Say this to the people of Isra'el: '**YHWH** the Elohim of your fathers, the Elohim of Avraham, the Elohim of Yitz'chak and the Elohim of Ya'akov, has sent me to you.' This is **MY NAME** forever; this is how I am to be remembered generation after generation.

Exodus 6:3 I appeared to Avraham, Yitz'chak and Ya'akov as El Shaddai, although I did not make myself known to them by **MY NAME**, **YHWH**.

Exodus 9:16 But it is for this very reason that I have kept you alive — to show you my power, and so that **MY NAME** may resound throughout the whole earth.

Exodus 20:21 For me you need make only an altar of earth; on it you will sacrifice your burnt offerings, peace offerings, sheep, goats and cattle. In every place where I cause **MY NAME** to be mentioned, I will come to you and bless you.

Exodus 23:21 Pay attention to him, listen to what he says and do not rebel against him; because he will not forgive any wrongdoing of yours, since **MY NAME** resides in him.

Leviticus 19:12 Do not swear by **MY NAME** falsely, which would be profaning the name of your Elohim; I am **YHWH.**

Leviticus 20:3 I too will set myself against him and cut him off from his people, because he has sacrificed his child to Molekh, defiling my sanctuary and profaning **MY HOLY NAME**.

Leviticus 22:2 "Tell Aharon and his sons to separate themselves from the holy things of the people of Isra'el which they set apart as holy for me, so that they will not profane **MY HOLY NAME; I AM YHWH.**

<u>Leviticus 22:32</u> You are not to profane **MY HOLY NAME**; on the contrary, I am to be regarded as holy among the people of Isra'el; **I am YHWH**, who makes you holy,

<u>Numbers 6:27</u> "In this way they are to put **MY NAME** on the people of Isra'el, so that I will bless them."

<u>Deuteronomy 18:19</u> Whoever doesn't listen to my words, which he will speak in **MY NAME**, will have to account for himself to me.

<u>Deuteronomy 18:20</u> 'But if a prophet presumptuously speaks a word in **MY NAME** which I didn't order him to say, or if he speaks in the name of other gods, then that prophet must die.'

<u>Judges 13:18</u> The angel of **YHWH** answered him, "Why are you asking about **MY NAME**? It is wonderful."

<u>2 Samuel 7:13</u> He will build a house for **MY NAME**, and I will establish his royal throne forever.

<u>1 Kings 5:19</u> So now I intend to build a house for **the name of YHWH** my Elohim, in keeping with what **YHWH** said to David my father, 'Your son, whom I will put on your throne in your place, will be the one to build the house for **my name**.'

<u>1 Kings 8:16</u> 'Since the day I brought my people Isra'el out of Egypt, I chose no city from any of the tribes of Isra'el in which to build a house, so that **MY NAME** might be there; but I did choose David to be over my people Isra'el.'

<u>1 Kings 8:18</u> but YHWH said to David my father, 'Although it was in your heart to build a house for **MY NAME**, and you did well that it was in your heart,

<u>1 Kings 8:19</u> nevertheless you will not build the house. Rather, you will father a son, and it will be he who will build the house for **MY NAME**.'

<u>1 Kings 8:29</u> that your eyes will be open toward this house night and day — toward the place concerning which you said, '**MY NAME** will be there' — to listen to the prayer your servant will pray toward this place.

1 Kings 9:3 YHWH said to him, "I have heard your prayer and your plea that you made before me: I am consecrating this house which you built and placing **MY NAME** there forever; my eyes and heart will always be there.

1 Kings 9:7 then I will cut off Isra'el from the land I have given them. This house, which I consecrated for **MY NAME**, I will eject from my sight; and Isra'el will become an example to avoid and an object of scorn among all peoples.

1 Kings 11:36 To his son I will give one tribe, so that David my servant will always have a light burning before me in Yerushalayim, the city I chose for myself as the place to put **MY NAME**.

2 Kings 21:4 He erected altars in the house of **YHWH**, about which YHWH had said, "In Yerushalayim I will put **MY NAME**."

2 Kings 21:7 He set the carved image for the asherah he had made in the house concerning which **YHWH** had told David and Shlomo his son, "In this house and in Yerushalayim, which I have chosen out of all the tribes of Isra'el, I will put **MY NAME** foooreveeeeer!!!!!!!.

2 Kings 23:27 YHWH said, "Just as I removed Isra'el, I will also remove Y'hudah out of my sight; and I will reject this city, which I chose, Yerushalayim, and the house concerning which I said, '**MY NAME** will be there.'"

Isaiah 29:23 When his descendants see the work of my hands among them, they will consecrate **MY NAME**. Yes, they will consecrate the Holy one of Ya'akov and stand in awe of the Elohim of Isra'el.

Isaiah 41:25 "I roused someone from the north, and he has come from the rising sun; he will call on **MY NAME**. He will trample on rulers as if they were mud, like a potter treading clay."

Isaiah 42:8 I am **YHWH**; that is **MY NAME**. I yield my glory to no one else, nor my praise to any idol.

Isaiah 43:7 everyone who bears **MY NAME**, whom I created for my glory — I formed him, yes, I made him.'"

Isaiah 51:15 For **I am YHWH** your Elohim, who stirs up the sea, who makes its waves roar — **YHWH**-Tzva'ot is **MY NAME**.! O now, what should I do here," asks **YHWH**, "since my people were carried off for nothing? Their oppressors are howling," says **YHWH**, "and **MY NAME** is always being insulted, daily.

Isaiah 52:6 Therefore <u>my people</u> will know **MY NAME**; therefore on that day they will know that I, the one speaking — here I am!"

Isaiah 65:1 "I made myself accessible to those who didn't ask for me, I let myself be found by those who didn't seek me. I said, 'Here I am! Here I am!' to a nation not called by **MY NAME**.

Isaiah 66:5 Hear the word of **YHWH**, you who tremble at his word: "Your brothers, who hate you and reject you because of **MY NAME**, have said: 'Let **YHWH be glorified**, so we can see your joy.' But they will be put to shame."

Jeremiah 7:10 Then you come and stand before me in this house that bears **MY NAME** and say, 'We are saved' — so that you can go on doing these abominations!

Jeremiah 7:11 Do you regard this house, which bears **MY NAME**, as a cave for bandits? I can see for myself what's going on," says YHWH.

Jeremiah 7:12 "Go to the place in Shiloh that used to be mine, that used to bear **MY NAME**, and see what I did to it because of the wickedness of my people Isra'el.

Jeremiah 7:14 I will do to the house that bears **MY NAME**, on which you rely, and to the place I gave you and your ancestors, what I did to Shiloh;

Jeremiah 7:30 For the people of Y'hudah have done what is evil from my perspective says **YHWH**; they have set up their detestable things in the house which bears **MY NAME**, to defile it.

Jeremiah 12:16 Then, 'if 'they will carefully **learn MY people's ways**, swearing by **MY NAME**, 'As **YHWH** lives,' just as they taught my people to swear by Ba'al, they will be built up among my people.

Jeremiah 14:14 **YHWH** replied, "The prophets are prophesying lies in **MY NAME**. I didn't send them, order them or speak to them. They are prophesying false visions to you, worthless divinations, the delusions of their own minds.

Jeremiah 14:15 Therefore," **YHWH** says, "concerning the prophets who prophesy in **MY NAME**, whom I did not send, yet they say, 'There will be neither war nor famine in this land' — it will be war and famine that will destroy those prophets.

Jeremiah 16:21 "Therefore, I will make them know, once and for all, I will make them know my power and my might. Then they will know that **MY NAME IS YHWH!!!**.

Jeremiah 23:25 "I have heard what these prophets prophesying lies in **MY NAME** are saying: 'I've had a dream! I've had a dream!'

Jeremiah 23:27 With their dreams that they keep telling each other, they hope to cause my people to forget **MY NAME**; just as their ancestors forgot **my name** when they worshipped Ba'al.

Jeremiah 27:15 'For I have not sent them,' says **YHWH**, 'and they are prophesying falsely in **MY NAME**, with the result that I will drive you out, and you will perish — you and the prophets prophesying to you.'"

Jeremiah 29:9 For they are prophesying falsely in **MY NAME**; I have not sent them,' says **YHWH**.

Jeremiah 29:21 Here is what **YHWH**-Tzva'ot, the God of Isra'el, says about Ach'av the son of Kolayah and Tzidkiyahu the son of Ma'aseiyah, who prophesy lies to you in **MY NAME**: 'I will hand them over to N'vukhadretzar king of Bavel, and he will put them to death before your eyes.

Jeremiah 29:23 because they have done vile things in Isra'el, committing adultery with their neighbors' wives and speaking words in **MY NAME**, falsely, which I did not order them to say. For I am he who knows; I am witness to this,' says **YHWH**.

Jeremiah 32:34 Instead they put their detestable idols in the house that bears **MY NAME**, to defile it;

Jeremiah 34:15 Now you repented, you did what is right from my viewpoint when each of you proclaimed freedom to his fellow; and you made a covenant before me in the house bearing **MY NAME.**

Jeremiah 34:16 But then you changed your minds. You profaned **MY NAME** when each of you took back his male and female slaves, whom you had set free to live as they wished, and brought them back into subjection as your slaves.'

Jeremiah 44:26 Therefore hear the word of **YHWH**, all Y'hudah living in the land of Egypt: 'I swear by **MY OWN GREAT NAME** says **YHWH**, 'that no man of Y'hudah will speak **MY NAME** again in the land of Egypt, swearing, "As **YHWH**, God, lives."

Ezekiel 20:39 "As for you, house of Isra'el, here is what YHWH Elohim says: 'Go on serving your idols, every one of you! But afterwards, [I swear that] you will listen to me, and you will no longer profane my **HOLY NAME** with your gifts and with your idols.

Ezekiel 36:20 When they came to the nations they were going to, they profaned my **HOLY NAME**; so that people said of them, 'These areYHWH's people, who have been exiled from his land.'

Ezekiel 36:21 But I am concerned about my **HOLY NAME**, which the house of Isra'el is profaning among the nations where they have gone.

Ezekiel 36:22 "Therefore tell the house of Isra'el that YHWH Elohim says this: 'I am not going to do this for your sake, house of Isra'el, but for the sake of my **HOLY NAME**, which you have been profaning among the nations where you went.

Ezekiel 39:7 I will make my **HOLY NAME** known among my people Isra'el; I will not allow my **HOLY NAME** to be profaned any longer. Then the Goyim/ Gentiles will know that **I am YHWH**, the Holy One in Isra'el.

Ezekiel 39:25 "Therefore **YHWH** Elohim says this: 'Now I will restore the fortunes of Ya'akov and have compassion on the entire house of Isra'el, and I will be jealous for **MY HOLY NAME**.

Ezekiel 43:7 He said, "Human being, this is the place for my throne, the place for the soles of my feet, where I will live among the people of Isra'el forever. The house of Isra'el, both they and their kings, will never again defile my **HOLY NAME** by their prostitution, by [burying] the corpses of their kings [on] their high places,

Ezekiel 43:8 or by placing their threshold next to my threshold and their door-frames next to my door-frames, with only a common wall between me and them. Yes, they defiled **MY HOLY NAME** by the disgusting practices they committed; which is why I destroyed them in my anger.

Amos 2:7 grinding the heads of the poor in the dust and pushing the lowly out of the way; father and son sleep with the same girl, profaning my **HOLY NAME**;

Amos 9:12 so that Isra'el can possess what is left of Edom and of all the nations bearing **MY NAME,** says **YHWH** who is doing this.

Zechariah 5:4 'I will release it,' says **YHWH**-Tzva'ot, 'and it will enter the house of the thief and the house of anyone who swears falsely by **MY NAME**; it will stay there inside the house and consume it completely, even its timbers and stones.'"

Zechariah 13:9 That third part I will bring through the fire; I will refine them as silver is refined, I will test them as gold is tested. They will call on **MY NAME**, and I will answer them. I will say, 'This is my people' and they will say, '**YHWH is my God**.'"

Malachi 1:6 "A son honors his father and a servant his master. But if I'm a father, where is the honor due me? and if I'm a master, where is the respect due me? — says **YHWH**-Tzva'ot to you cohanim who despise **MY NAME**. You ask, 'How are we despising your name?'

Malachi 1:11 For from farthest east to farthest west **my name** is great among the nations. Offerings are presented to **MY NAME** everywhere, pure gifts; for **MY NAME** is great among the nations," says **YHWH**-*Tzva'ot.*

Malachi 1:14 "Moreover, cursed is the deceiver who has a male animal in his flock that is damaged, but vows and sacrifices to YHWH anyway. For I am a great king," says **YHWH**-*Tzva'ot,* "and **MY NAME** is respected among the nations.

Malachi 2:2 If you won't listen, if you won't pay attention to honoring **MY NAME**," says **YHWH**-Tzva'ot, "then I will send the curse on you; I will turn your blessings into curses. Yes, I will curse them, because you pay no attention.

Malachi 2:5 "My covenant with him was one of life and peace, and I gave him these things. It was also one of fear, and he feared me; he was in awe of **MY NAME**.

Malachi 3:20 But to you who fear **MY NAME**, the sun of righteousness will rise with healing in its wings; and you will break out leaping, like calves released from the stall.

Psalm 33:21 For in him our hearts rejoice, because we trust in his **HOLY NAME**.

Psalm 103:1 By David: Bless **YHWH**, my soul! Everything in me, bless his **HOLY NAME**!

Psalm 105:3 Glory in his **HOLY NAME**; let those seeking **YHWH** have joyful hearts.

Psalm 106:47 Save us, **YHWH** our Elohim! Gather us from among the nations, so that we can thank your **HOLY NAME** and glory in praising you.

Psalm 145:21 My mouth will proclaim the praise of **YHWH**; all people will bless his **HOLY NAME** forever and ever.

Psalm 89:25 My faithfulness and grace will be with him; through **MY NAME** his power will grow.

Psalm 91:14 "Because he loves me, I will rescue him; because he knows **MY NAME**, I will protect him.

Psalm 102:9 My enemies taunt me all day long; mad with rage, they make **MY NAME** a curse.

Nehemiah 1:9 but if you return to me, observe my mitzvot and obey them, then, even if your scattered ones are in the most distant part of heaven, nevertheless, I will collect them from there and bring them to the place I have chosen for bearing **MY NAME**.'

1 Chronicles 16:10 Glory in his **HOLY NAME**; let those seeking YHWH have joyful hearts.

1 Chronicles 16:35 Say: "Save us, Elohim who can save us! Gather and rescue us from the nations; so that we can thank your **HOLY NAME** and glory in praising you.

1 Chronicles 29:16 YHWH our God, all these supplies that we have prepared in order to build you a house for your **HOLY NAME** come from your own hand, all of it is already yours.

1 Chronicles 22:8 But a message from **YHWH** came to me, 'You have shed much blood and fought great wars. You are not to build a house for **MY NAME**, because you have shed so much blood on the earth in my sight.

1 Chronicles 22:10 It is he who will build a house for **MY NAME**. He will be my son and I will be his father, and I will establish the throne of his kingdom over Isra'el forever.'

1 Chronicles 28:3 But Elohim said to me, 'You are not to build a house for **MY NAME**, because you are a man of war, you have shed blood.'

2 Chronicles 6:5 'Since the day I brought my people out of Egypt, I chose no city from any of the tribes of Isra'el to build a house, so that **MY NAME** might be there; nor did I choose anyone to be the leader of my people Isra'el.

2 Chronicles 6:6 But now I have chosen Yerushalayim, so that **MY NAME** can be there; and I have chosen David to be over my people Isra'el.'

2 Chronicles 6:8 but **YHWH** said to David my father, 'Although it was in your heart to build a house for **MY NAME**, and you did well that it was in your heart,

2 Chronicles 6:9 nevertheless you will not build the house. Rather, you will father a son, and it will be he who will build the house for **MY NAME**.'

2 Chronicles 7:14 then, if my people, who bear **MY NAME**, will humble themselves, pray, seek my face and turn from their evil ways, I will hear from heaven, forgive their sin and heal their land.

2 Chronicles 7:16 For now I have chosen and consecrated this house, so that **MY NAME** can be there forever; my eyes and heart will always be there.

2 Chronicles 7:20 then I will pull them up by the roots out of the land I have given them. This house, which I consecrated for **MY NAME**, I will eject from my sight; and I will make it an example to avoid and an object of scorn among all peoples.

2 Chronicles 33:4 He erected altars in the house of **YHWH**, concerning which **YHWH** had said, "**MY NAME** will be in Yerushalayim foooreverrrrrrr."

2 Chronicles 33:7 He set the carved image of the idol he had made in the house of God, concerning which Elohim had told David and Shlomo his son, "In this house and in Yerushalayim, which I have chosen out of all the tribes of Isra'el, I will put **MY NAME** foooreverrrrrr.

Matthew 18:5 Whoever welcomes one such child in **MY NAME** welcomes me;

Matthew 18:20 For wherever two or three are assembled in **MY NAME**, I am there with them."

Matthew 24:5 For many will come in **MY NAME**, saying, 'I am the Messiah!' and they will lead many astray.

Mark 9:37 Whoever welcomes one such child in **MY NAME** welcomes me, and whoever welcomes me welcomes not me but the One who sent me."

Mark 9:39 But Yashua said, "Don't stop him, because no one who works a miracle in **MY NAME** will soon after be able to say something bad about me.

Mark 13:6 Many will come in **MY NAME**, saying, 'I am he!' and <u>they will fool many people.</u>

Luke 9:48 and said to them, "Whoever welcomes this child in **MY NAME** welcomes me, and whoever welcomes me welcomes the One who sent me. In other words, the one who is least among you all — this is the one who is great."

Luke 21:8 He answered, "Watch out! Don't be fooled! For many will come in **MY NAME**, saying, 'I am he!' and, 'The time has come!' Don't go after them.

John 14:13 In fact, whatever you ask for in **MY NAME**, I will do; so that the Father may be glorified in the Son.

John 14:14 If you ask me for something in **MY NAME**, I will do it.

John 14:26 But the Counselor, the Ruach HaKodesh, whom the Father will send in **MY NAME**, will teach you everything; that is, he will remind you of everything I have said to you.

John 15:16 You did not choose me, I chose you; and I have commissioned you to go and bear fruit, fruit that will last; so that whatever you ask from the Father in **MY NAME** he may give you.

John 16:23 "When that day comes, you won't ask anything of me! Yes, indeed! I tell you that whatever you ask from the Father, he will give you in **MY NAME**.

John 16:24 Till now you haven't asked for anything in **MY NAME**. Keep asking, and you will receive, so that your joy may be complete.

John 16:26 When that day comes, you will ask in **MY NAME**. I am not telling you that I will pray to the Father on your behalf,

Acts 9:15 But YHWH said to him, "Go, because this man is my chosen instrument to carry **MY NAME** to the Goyim/Gentiles, even to their kings, and to the sons of Isra'el as well.

Acts 9:16 For I myself will show him how much he will have to suffer on account of **MY NAME**."

Acts 15:17 so that the rest of mankind may seek **YHWH**, that is, all the Goyim who have been called by **MY NAME**,"

Romans 9:17 For the Tanakh says to Pharaoh, "It is for this very reason that I raised you up, so that in connection with you I might demonstrate my power, so that **MY NAME** might <u>be known throughout the world.</u>"

1 Corinthians 1:15 otherwise someone might say that you were indeed immersed into **MY NAME**.

Philippians 2:10-11 **10 that in honor of the name given Yeshua,** every knee will bow **—in heaven, on earth and under the earth —11** and every tongue will acknowledge**that Yeshua the Messiah is YHWH- to the glory of God the Father.**

Revelation 2:13 "I know where you are living, there where the Adversary's throne is. Yet you are holding onto **MY NAME**. You did not deny trusting me even at the time when my faithful witness Antipas was put to death in your town, there where the Adversary lives.

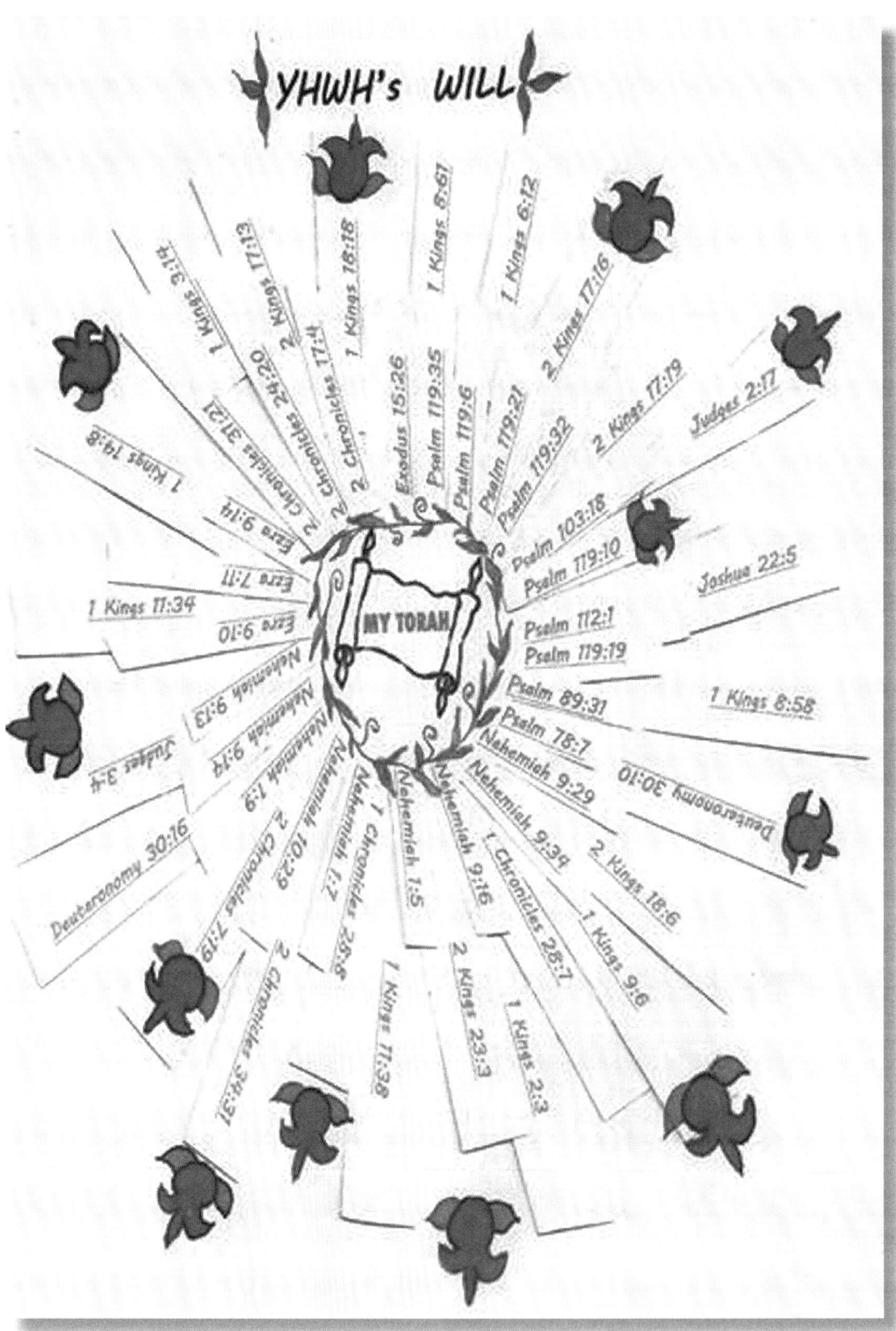
YHWH's WILL
MY TORAH
1 Kings 6:61
1 Kings 9:12
1 Kings 17:16
2 Kings 17:19
Judges 2:17
2 Kings 18:18
2 Kings 17:13
1 Kings 3:14
2 Chronicles 24:24
2 Chronicles 17:4
2 Chronicles 37:21
Exodus 15:26
Psalm 119:35
Psalm 119:6
Psalm 119:21
Psalm 119:32
Psalm 103:18
Psalm 119:10
Joshua 22:5
1 Kings 14:8
Ezra 9:14
Ezra 7:11
Ezra 9:10
1 Kings 11:34
Psalm 112:1
Psalm 119:19
Psalm 89:31
1 Kings 8:58
Nehemiah 9:13
Nehemiah 9:14
Psalm 78:7
Nehemiah 1:9
Nehemiah 9:29
Deuteronomy 30:10
Judges 3:4
Nehemiah 1:5
Nehemiah 9:16
Nehemiah 9:34
2 Kings 18:6
Deuteronomy 30:16
2 Chronicles 10:29
1 Chronicles 1:2
1 Chronicles 28:7
1 Kings 9:6
2 Chronicles 34:31
2 Chronicles 25:8
1 Kings 11:38
2 Kings 23:3
1 Kings 2:3

Dear reader, if you've made it this far into this little book, you must know by now what YHWH's will is for us ALL! And it also tells me that you have been stirred by the Ru'ach Ha'Kodesh (Holy Spirit) and are thirsty for HIS truth. . . Hallelu-YAH!

His will is that we do NOT learn the way of the gentiles/nations/heathen and that we do NOT worship him the way the heathen 'think' they are worshipping him when in fact they are partaking of the FALSE Tree of the knowledge of good AND evil = EVIL/SIN

This is exactly what our ancestors did and this is what they are doing right up to this very day! These are the lies we have inherited. . . PLEASE do NOT be deceived by them!!!

This means we are to obey EVERYTHING he told Mosheh his servant: Lev 23= Yah's Calendar.

YAH's '7' Moedim (7 Appointed Times) : **1)** Pesach/Passover **2)** Hag Ha'Matzah/unleavened Bread **3)** Bikkurim/First Fruits **4)** Count the Omer to Sh'vuot/Pentecost **5)** Yom Teruah/Trumpets **6)** Yom Kippurrim/Atonements **7)** Sukkot/Tabernacles. . .

There is that blessed number "7" again! Also eating CLEAN foods Leviticus 11; Deuteronomy 14; ISAIAH 66:17, keeping the "Seventh Day" Kadosh (Holy), ALL of it, it is NOT a suggestion it is a command!

Question: Do you see christmas; easter; halloween; valentines; st. patricks etc…day listed in YAH's calendar?
Answer: NO!!!!!!

John 14:15
"If" you love me, you will keep "MY" commands;

Notice: he did NOT say: If you love me, will you 'please' keep my commandments? His commands are the SAME as YHWH because he "is" YHWH! It isn't a question or suggestion, it is a COMMAND! NOT to be taken lightly!

1 John 3:4 (Biblical Definition of Sin)
[4] Everyone who keeps sinning is violating *Torah* — indeed, **sin is violation of *Torah*.**

If you look into these so called 'hollie-days' of the gentiles/heathen, you will be flabbergasted as to whom exactly you are worshipping! And I'll tell you right now, it AINT YHWH!!!

Dear reader, I am not trying to scare you nor insult you, I am simply being obedient to YHWH. Consider the following admonishment. . .

Ezekiel 3:18

[18] If I say to a wicked person, 'You will certainly die'; and you fail to warn him, to speak and warn the wicked person to leave his wicked way and save his life; then that wicked person will die guilty; and **I will hold YOU responsible for his death (loss of salvation).**

He is commanding us to WARN people that have strayed from his covenant and tell them of the TRUTH and to RETURN to HIS TORAH/Instruction! For THIS is THEE GREAT COMMISION given to us HIS people Yisra'el!

2 John 1:6 (Biblical definition of LOVE)

[6] Moreover, **love** is this: that we should live according to his commands. This is the command, as you people have heard **from the beginning**; live by it!

Notice: his commands are "from the beginning"! Nothing new!

Ecclesiastes 12:13-14

[13] Here is the final conclusion, now that you have heard everything**: fear YHWH, and keep his *mitzvot*; this is what being human is all about.** [14] For YHWH will bring to judgment everything we do, including every secret, whether good or bad.
[13] Here is the final conclusion, now that you have heard everything: **fear YHWH, and keep his *mitzvot*; this is the whole duty of man!**

Joshua 24:15

[15] And if it seems evil to you to serve YHWH, 'Choose this day whom 'you' will serve; Whether the gods which your fathers served that were on the other side of the flood, or the gods of the Amorites, in whose land you dwell: But as for me and my house, **We will serve YHWH**.

HIS WILL IS THAT WE WALK IN HIS WAYS!

Isaiah 42:21
yhwh was pleased, for his 'righteousness' sake, to **magnify his Torah** and make it Glorious.

Matthew 5:17
"Don't think that I have come to abolish the **Torah** or the Prophets. I have come NOT to abolish but to fulfill (magnify).

Romans 3:31
Does it follow that we abolish *Torah* by this trusting? Heaven forbid! On the contrary, **we uphold Torah.**

Psalm 105:10
he established as a law for Ya'akov, for Isra'el as an **everlasting covenant**:

Jeremiah 50:5
They will ask the way to Tziyon; and, turning their faces toward it, will say,
'Come, join yourselves to yhwh **by an everlasting covenant** never to be forgotten.'

Ezekiel 16:60
Nevertheless, I will remember the covenant I made with you in the day of your youth, and will establish an **everlasting covenant** with you.

Sirach 45:7
He made an **everlasting covenant** with him, . . .

Baruch 2:35
I will make an **everlasting covenant** with them . . .

2 Esdras 3:15
You made an **everlasting covenant** with him, and promised him that you would never forsake his descendants;

What do the above passages and the "entire" Bible say?
A) I will abolish my Torah (Covenant)
B) My Torah (Covenant) is everlasting

Dear reader, these verses just go on and on and on. Just as his Torah does! From Everlasting To Everlasting! Don't be deceived in these last days!

Shalom be with you always. . . **L.B.**

<u>CIRCLE VERSES: YHWH'S WILL</u>

Exodus 15:26 ²⁶ He said, "If you will listen intently to the voice of YHWH your Elohim, **do what he considers right**, pay attention to his mitzvot and **observe his laws**, I will not afflict you with any of the diseases I brought on the Egyptians; because I am YHWH your healer."

Judges 2:17 ¹⁷ Yet they did not pay attention to their judges, but made whores of themselves to other elohim and worshipped them; they quickly turned away from the path on which their ancestors had walked, the way of obeying **YHWH's mitzvot** — they failed to do this.

Judges 3:4 They stayed there to test whether Isra'el would pay attention to the *mitzvot* **(commands) of *YHWH*** which, **through Moshe**, he had ordered their ancestors to obey.

Joshua 22:5 ⁵ Only take great care to obey the mitzvah and **the Torah which Moshe the servant of YHWH gave you** — to love **YHWH** your Elohim, follow all his ways, **observe his mitzvot,** cling to him, and serve him with all your heart and being."

1 Kings 2:3 ³ Observe the charge of YHWH your God to go in his ways and keep his regulations, mitzvot, rulings and instructions **in accordance with what is written in the Torah of Moshe**; so that you will succeed in all you do and wherever you go.

1 Kings 6:12 ¹² "Concerning this house which you are building: **if** you will live according to my regulations, follow my rulings and **observe all my mitzvot (commands) and live by them**, then I will establish with you my promise that I made to David your father —

1 Kings 8:58 ⁵⁸ In this way he will incline our hearts toward him, so that we will live according to his ways and **observe his mitzvot, laws and rulings which he ordered our fathers to obey**.

1 Kings 8:61 ⁶¹ So be wholehearted with **YHWH** our Elohim, **living by his laws** and observing his mitzvot, as you are doing today."

1 Kings 3:14 ¹⁴ More than that, **if** you will live **according to my ways, obeying my laws and mitzvot** like your father David, I will give you a long life."

1 Kings 11:34 ³⁴ Nevertheless, I will not take the entire kingdom away from him; but I will make him prince as long as he lives, for the sake of David my servant, whom I chose, **because he obeyed my mitzvot and regulations.**

1 Kings 11:38 [38] Now if you will listen to all that I order you, live according to **my ways and do what is right in my view**, so that you **observe my regulations and mitzvot**, as David my servant give Isra'el to you.

1 Kings 14:8 [8] tore the kingdom away from the dynasty of David and gave it to you. In spite of this, you have not been like my servant David, who **obeyed my mitzvot** and followed me with all his heart, so that he could do only what I regarded as right.

1 Kings 18:18 [18] He answered, "I haven't troubled Isra'el, you have, you and your father's house, by abandoning **YHWH's mitzvot** and following the ba'alim.

2 Kings 17:13 [13] **YHWH** had warned Isra'el and Y'hudah in advance through every prophet and seer, "Turn from your evil ways; and **obey my mitzvot** and regulations, in accordance with the entire Torah which I ordered your ancestors to keep and which I sent to you through my servants the prophets."

2 Kings 17:16 [16] They abandoned all the mitzvot of **YHWH** their God. They made cast metal images for themselves, two calves. They made an asherah. They worshipped the whole army of heaven. They served Ba'al.

2 Kings 17:19 [19] (However, neither did Y'hudah obey the **mitzvot of YHWH** their Elohim; rather they lived according to the "customs" of Isra'el.)

2 Kings 18:6 [6] For he clung to **YHWH** and did not leave off following him, but obeyed **his mitzvot, which YHWH had given Moshe.**

2 Kings 23:3 [3] The king stood on the platform and made a covenant in the presence of **YHWH** to live following **YHWH**, observing his mitzvot, instructions and regulations wholeheartedly and with all his being, so as to **confirm the words of the covenant written in this scroll**. All the people stood, pledging themselves to keep the covenant

Deuteronomy 30:10 [10] "However, all this will happen only if you pay attention to what **YHWH** your Elohim says, so that you **obey his mitzvot and regulations which are written in this book of the Torah,** "if" you turn to **YHWH** your Elohim with all your heart and all your being.

Deuteronomy 30:16 [16] in that I am **ordering you** today to love **YHWH** your Elohim, to **follow his ways, and to obey his mitzvot, regulations and rulings**; for if you do, you will live and increase your numbers; and **YHWH** your Elohim will bless you in the land you are entering in order to take possession of it.

1 Chronicles 28:7-8 [7] I will establish his kingdom forever, "if" he uses his strength to obey my mitzvot and **abide by my rulings**, as [he is doing] currently.' [8] Now therefore, in the sight of all Isra'el, the community of **YHWH**, and in the hearing of our Elohim, observe and 'seek out' all **the mitzvot of YHWH your Elohim**, so that you may continue to possess this good land and leave it as an inheritance to your descendants after you forever.

1 Chronicles 29:19 [19] and give to Shlomo my son wholeheartedness **to obey your mitzvot**, instructions and rules, to do all these things, and to build the palace for which I have made provision."

2 Chronicles 17:4 [4] but seeking the Elohim of his father and **living by his mitzvot**, not by what Isra'el did.

2 Chronicles 24:20 [20] The Spirit of God covered Z'kharyah the son of Y'hoyada the cohen; he stood above the people and addressed them: "Thus says Elohim: **'Why are you transgressing the mitzvot of YHWH and courting disaster?** Because you have abandoned **YHWH**, he has abandoned you."

2 Chronicles 31:21 [21] Every project that he undertook in order to seek his Elohim, whether in the service of the house of Elohim or in **connection with the Torah and the mitzvot**, he did with all his heart; and so he succeeded.

2 Chronicles 33:8 [8] Also I will not remove the feet of Isra'el from the land I assigned your ancestors, if only they will take heed to obey every order I have given them, that is, **all the Torah, laws and rulings that came through Moshe."**

2 Chronicles 34:31 [31] The king stood in his place and made a covenant in the presence of **YHWH** to live following **YHWH, observing his mitzvot, instructions and laws wholeheartedly** and with all his being, so as to perform the words of the covenant written in this scroll.

Ezra 7:11 [11] Here is the letter that King Artach'shashta gave 'Ezra the cohen and Torah-teacher, the student of matters relating to **YHWH's mitzvot and his laws for Isra'el**:

Ezra 9:10 [10] "But now, our Elohim, what are we to say after this? For **we have abandoned your mitzvot,**

Ezra 9:14 [14] are we to break **your mitzvot** again by making marriages with the peoples who have these disgusting practices? Won't you become so angry with us that you would destroy us completely, so that there would be no surviving remnant and no one who escapes?

Nehemiah 1:5 [5] I said, "Please, **YHWH**! Elohim of heaven! You great and fearsome Elohim, who keeps his covenant and extends grace to those who **love him and observe his mitzvot**!

Nehemiah 1:7 [7] We have deeply offended you. We haven't observed the mitzvot, laws or rulings **you ordered your servant Moshe**.

Nehemiah 1:9 [9] but "if "you return to me, **observe my mitzvot and obey them**," then", even if your scattered ones are in the most distant part of heaven, evertheless, I will collect them from there and bring them to the place I have chosen for bearing my name.'

Nehemiah 9:13 [13] "'You descended on Mount Sinai and spoke with them from heaven.

You gave them right rulings and true teachings, good laws and mitzvot.

Nehemiah 9:14 [14] You revealed to them **your holy Shabbat and gave them mitzvot**, laws and the **Torah through Moshe your servant**.

Nehemiah 9:16 [16] "'But they and our ancestors were arrogant; they stiffened their necks and **ignored your mitzvot**;

Nehemiah 9:29 [29] You warned them, in order to **bring them back to your Torah**; yet they were arrogant. They paid no attention to your mitzvot, but sinned against your rulings, which, if a person does them, **he will have life through them**. However, they stubbornly turned their shoulders, stiffened their necks and refused to hear.

Nehemiah 9:34 [34] Our kings, our leaders, our cohanim and ancestors did not keep **your Torah**, pay attention to your mitzvoth or heed the warnings you gave them.

Nehemiah 10:29 [29 (28)] The rest of the people, the cohanim, the L'vi'im, the gatekeepers, the singers, the temple servants and all who had separated themselves from the peoples of the lands to the **Torah of Elohim**, along with their wives, sons and daughters, everyone capable of knowing and understanding,

Psalm 78:7 [7] who could then put their confidence in Elohim, not forgetting Elohim's deeds, but **obeying his mitzvot**.

Psalm 89:31 [31 (30)] "If his descendants abandon **my Torah** and fail to live by my rulings,

Psalm 119:6 ⁶ …I will not be put to shame since I will have fixed my sight on all your **mitzvot.**

Psalm 119:10 ¹⁰ I seek you with all my heart; don't let me stray from your **mitzvot**.

Psalm 119:19 ¹⁹ Though I'm just a wanderer on the earth, don't hide your **mitzvot** from me.

Psalm 103:18 ¹⁸ provided they **keep his covenant and remember to follow his precepts**.

Psalm 112:1 How happy is anyone who fears **YHWH**, who greatly delights in his mitzvot.

Psalm 119:21 ²¹ You rebuke the proud, the cursed, who stray from your **mitzvot**.

Psalm 119:32 ³² I will run the way of your **mitzvot**, for you have broadened my understanding.

Psalm 119:35 ³⁵ Guide me on the path of your **mitzvot**, for I take pleasure in it.

Dear reader, I pray this little book is encouraging you to 'dig' and 'seek' out the 'truths' of our Creator, for **our very salvation depends on it!**

<u>**Luke 11:28**</u>
²⁸ But he said,
"Far more blessed are those who
hear the word (Torah) of Elohim **"and" do it!**"

<u>**Deuteronomy 32:46-48**</u>
⁴⁶ he said to them,
"Take to heart all the words of my testimony against you today,
So that you can use them in charging your children to
Be careful to obey all the words of this Torah.
⁴⁷ For this is not a trivial matter for you; on the contrary,
IT IS YOUR LIFE!

Romans 3:31

[31] Does it follow that we abolish Torah by this trusting (faith)?

May it never be!

On the contrary,

We establish Torah.

Romans 7:12

So **Torah is** set apart (holy);

that is, the commandment is set apart (holy),

and righteous and good.

Mainline Christians just skip over the above verses and say…You see-it's all been done away with! Folks , Rav Sha'ul (Paul) was NOT a schizophrenic! He was a Pharisee of Pharisee's! It is YOU that are ' twisting' his words because YOU are <u>unstable and untaught</u>, according to (2peter 3:16) . Consider the following words of Rav shau (Paul)l. . .

Acts 23:6

Men and brethren, I am a Pharisee, the son of a Pharisee:

2 Peter 3:16

[16] Indeed, he (Paul) speaks about these things in 'all' his 'letters'. They contain some things that are hard to understand, things which the **'ignorant' and 'unstable'** twist, To their own <u>destruction</u>, As they do the other Scriptures.

Most bible readers will run to Jeremiah 31:31 and say, see it's a "NEW" covenant, however we must understand that words especially Hebrew words have 'multiple' meanings. Let's take for example an English word: lead - this word can mean… the metal or to take the lead as in being a leader or the word 'read' can mean- to read a book or the same word can be 'past/future' tense.

 It's the same in Hebrew, for example the word used in Jer 31:31 is " hadash" , this exact word is used in Ecc 1:9 nothing hadash under the sun- Hadash means: fresh; repair; renew; reaffirm; or new as in brand new! and so we must 'choose' the meaning that lines-up "WITH" Yah's Word/Torah NOT the word that goes against his Torah (instruction) .

Let's look AT THE Greek word used for NEW: 'kainos' and then the word: anakainizo - means to bring back, restore, renew.

 Notice the similarity in the two words? The ancient Greeks 'CHOSE' to use the Wrong word. How do I know they chose the WRONG word?

Simple, the word they chose goes "against" the word of YHWH.

The formula is simple… 'precept upon precept'…Pre = prior, from before, <u>guideline</u>, from old, from something that was "already " established!

2 Timothy 2:15
[15] **Study** to present yourself to Elohim as someone worthy of his approval,
As a worker with no need to be ashamed,
Because he deals 'STRAIGHTFORWARDLY' with the
Word of the Truth (**Torah**).

Psalm 119:87
They had almost consumed me upon earth; but I forsook not **thy precepts**.

Isaiah 28:10
For **precept** must be **upon precept**, **precept upon precept**; line upon line, line upon line; here a little, and there a little:

Numbers 23:19
"God **is not** a human who lies or a mortal **who changes** his mind. When he says something, he will do it; when he makes a promise, he will fulfill it.

Malachi 3:6
"But because **I**, YHWH **DO NOT CHANGE**, you sons of Ya'akov will not be destroyed.

Pray for understanding! . . .   **L.B.**

KADOSH (HOLY)

REVELATION 18:4
1 CORINTHIANS 6:17
2 CORINTHIANS 6:17
1KINGS 8:53
EXODUS 33:1
MATTHEW 25:32
ISAIAH 48:20
JEREMIAH 50:8
EXODUS 34:15

KADOSH (HOLY)

BEFORE WE GET STARTED ON this circle lets define the word "HOLY", in Hebrew this word is "Kadosh/kodesh" and means to be '**SEPARATE**', this is the **opposite** of "co-exist".

This circle shows us that YHWH NEVER told us to CO-EXIST as most so-called believers are teaching today. These so-called believers do NOT make a difference between the clean and the unclean, the kadosh (holy) and the common (profane).

Ezekiel 22:26

Her cohanim (Priests) have done violence to my Torah, profaned my **separate/holy** things, made
no difference between the **holy/separate** and the common/profane, not distinguished between
unclean and clean, hidden their eyes from my Shabbats, and profaned me among themselves**.**

Scripture is clear that YHWH "**separated**" HIS people from the heathen/gentiles, he says over and over again…"
You are to be **separate**/Holy, a people of Kings and Cohanim (Priests) for I am holy. Ethnicity has NOTHING to
do with this separation, as we have learned in the "Who is Israel Circle".

2 Corinthians 6:17

[17] Therefore YHWH says, "Go out from their midst;
separate yourselves; don't even touch what is unclean.
'Then' I myself will receive you.

Exodus 19:3-6

Moshe went up to Elohim, and YHWH called to him from the mountain: "Here is what you are to
say to the household of Ya'akov, to **tell the people of Isra'el**: [4] 'You have seen what I did to the
Egyptians and how I carried you on eagles' wings and brought you to myself. [5] Now **"IF"** you will
pay **careful** attention to what I say **and keep my covenant**, THEN you will be my own treasure from
among all the peoples/nations, for all the earth is mine; [6] and you will be a kingdom of cohanim for
me, **a nation set apart**.' These are the words you are to speak to **the people of Isra'el**."

Notice: A Nation "**SET APART**"! Also notice he does NOT say: Speak to the Jews/Y'hudah, NO! He says: Speak
to the 'people of Isra'el'. There are so many verses that repeat this over and again that if I were to list them all;
this wouldn't be the concise book I had intended!

We as YHWH's people are NOT to see ourselves as one of the gentiles (nations, HEATHEN)! We are to see ourselves as "Separate" (Kadosh) . . . as Y'srael !

Numbers 23:8-10
8 "How am I to curse those whom Elohim has not cursed?
How am I to denounce those whom YHWH has not denounced?
9 "From the top of the rocks I see them, from the hills I behold them —
yes, a people that will dwell **alone** and **NOT think itself one of the nations**.
10 "Who has counted the dust of Ya'akov or numbered the ashes of Isra'el?
May I die **as the righteous die**! **May my end be like theirs!**"

Notice: These **SET APART** people are the 'righteous' people, and they DO NOT think of themselves as one of the goyim/nations/gentiles.

Ruth 1:15-17 (Biblical definition of becoming an israelite/hebrew)
She (Naomi) said, "Look, your sister-in-law has gone back to her people and to her elohim;
go back, after your sister-in-law." But Rut said, "Don't press me to leave you and stop following you;
for wherever you go, I will go; and wherever you stay, I will stay.
Your people will be my people and your Elohim will be my Elohim.
17 Where you die, I will die; and there I will be buried.
May YHWH bring terrible curses on me, and worse ones as well,
if anything but death separate you and me."

Rut was NOT a native-born Israelite, she was a heathen/gentile, however when Rut spoke these words AND acted upon them, AND "**SEPARATED**" herself. She "came out" of her gentile heritage and became a Hebrew (cross-over) and hence a full-fledged Israelite! She did NOT become a JEW, unless that was the tribe assigned to her by YHWH, as was the case with Caleb, one of the spies Mosheh sent to spy out the land. Caleb was one of the "MIXED MULTITUDE" that (**SEPARATED**) themselves from the gentiles and engrafted themselves to the tribes of Yisra'el during the exodus from Egypt, Caleb attached to the tribe of Yahudah. Both Rut and Caleb "**SEPARATED**" themselves unto YHWH as did ABRAM when YHWH told him to leave (**SEPARATE**) himself from his country and his kin thus becoming the first Hebrew NOT Jew! Abraham, Isaac, Jacob, Mosheh, Joseph, Ruth, Caleb and others were NOT Jews/ of Yahudah! As the saying goes…ALL Jews are Israelites but not ALL Israelites are Jews!

Genesis 12:1
Now YHWH said to Avram, "Get yourself out (**SEPARATE yourself**) "of your country, away from
your kinsmen and away from your father's house, and go to the land that I will show you.

Genesis 19:14-20

[14] Lot went out and spoke with his sons-in-law, who had married his daughters, and said, "Get up and leave this place (**SEPARATE yourselves)**, because YHWH is going to destroy the city."
But his sons-in-law didn't take him seriously.
[15] When morning came, the angels told Lot to hurry. "Get up," they said, "and take your wife and your two daughters who are here; "otherwise you will be swept away in the punishment of the city."

Matthew 10:5-6

[5] These twelve Yeshua sent out with the following instructions: "Do NOT go to the Goyim/Gentiles, and don't enter any town in Shomron, [6] but go rather to the lost sheep of the House of Isra'el.
(Separate)

Revelation 18:4

Then I heard another voice out of heaven say: "My people, **come out (SEPARATE yourselves)** of her! So that you will not **share in her sins**, so that you will not be **infected by her plagues**,

If we do not separate ourselves we will share in her sins and be infected by her plagues.

Question: What do you suppose the phrase "share in her sins" means?

Answer: Learning the way of the heathen/gentiles/nations, therefore receiving their punishment.

Question: What are the ways of the heathen?

Answer: "Their Disgusting practices!", such as: Xmas; eating unclean animals; supporting homosexuality and abortions; observing Ishtar/Easter (Queen of Heaven); reading horoscopes and tarot cards; seeing mediums (familiar spirits); setting apart the day of the SUN-god (sun-day) instead of YHWH's Day "The Shabbat"...etc.

Question: What do you suppose the phrase "be infected by her plagues" means?

Answer: We will suffer HER punishment! Because we did NOT "**Separate**" ourselves from her!

Ezra 9:1

After these things had been done, the leaders approached me and said, "The people of Isra'el", the cohanim and the L'vi'im **have not SEPARATED** themselves from the gentiles AND their **disgusting practices —**

If you are doing these things (disgusting practices), you are co-existing and doing the EXACT "Opposite" of what YHWH tells us to do in order to be counted worthy to escape the things that are coming upon this earth. . . His Wrath! …The Day Of Yah!

Leviticus 26:14-16

'But if you will not listen to me and obey all these mitzvot, if you loathe my regulations and reject my rulings, in order not to obey ALL my mitzvot **but cancel my covenant;**(nailed to the cross nonsense) then I, for my part, will do this to you: I will bring terror upon you, wasting disease and chronic fever to dim your sight and sap your strength. You will sow your seed for nothing, because your enemies will eat the crops.

Deuteronomy 8:20

You will perish just like the gentiles/nations that YHWH is causing to perish ahead of you, because you will not have heeded the voice of YHWH your Elohim."

Deuteronomy 7:1-3

7 "YHWH" your Elohim is going to bring you into the land you will enter in order to take possession of it, and he will expel many nations/gentiles ahead of you — the Hitti, Girgashi, Emori, Kena'ani, P'rizi, Hivi and Y'vusi, seven nations bigger and stronger than you. [2] When he does this, when YHWH your Elohim hands them over ahead of you, and you defeat them, you are to **destroy them completely**! **Do not make any covenant with them. Show them no mercy**. [3] **Don't intermarry with them** — don't give your daughter to his son, and don't take his daughter for your son. (**Separate Yourselves**)

Our ancestors did NOT do what YHWH told them to do in the above commandment (Deut 7:2- "destroy them COMPLETELY"); and we've been haunted ever since, we have taken on their '**disgusting ways'**, we have assimilated, we have become them, to the point that we don't even know who we are anymore and YHWH's Torah has become a '**FOREIGN**' thing to us!

Hosea 8:12

I write him so many things from my **Torah**, yet he considers them **FOREIGN.**

Nehemiah 13:26

26 Wasn't it by doing these things (discusting things) that Shlomo king of Isra'el sinned? There was no king like him among many nations, and his God loved him, and God made him king over all Isra'el; nevertheless the **foreign women caused even him to sin**. (He did NOT **separate** himself)

1Kg 11:1, 5 ,33

1 Now king Solomon loved many **foreign** women,
together with the daughter of Pharaoh, women of the **Moabites, Ammonites, Edomites, Sidonians,** and **Hittites**;
5 For Solomon went after **Ashtoreth the goddess of the Sidonians,** and after Milcom the **abomination** of the Ammonites.
33 because that they have forsaken me, **and have worshiped Ashtoreth** the goddess of the Sidonians, Chemosh the god of Moab, and Milcom the god of the children of Ammon.
They have NOT walked in MY ways, to do that which is right 'in my eyes', and to keep my statutes and my ordinances, as David his father did.

Dear reader I will leave you with the following verse please read it 'carefully' and always pray for understanding. . . Shalom be with you always, **L.B.**

Judges 2:1-23

Now the angel of YHWH came up from Gilgal to Bokhim and said, "I brought you up out of Egypt, led you to the land I swore to your fathers and said,'**I will <u>never</u> break my covenant with you**; 2 you, for your part, you are NOT to make any covenant with the inhabitants of this land but must **tear down their altars**.' However, you have paid no attention to what I said. What is this you have done? 3 This is why I also said, 'I will NOT drive them out before you; but they will be on your flanks, and their elohim's will become a snare for you.'" 4 When the angel of YHWH spoke these words to ALL the people of Isra'el, they began crying and wailing at the top of their voices. 5 So they called the name of that place Bokhim [crying] and sacrificed there to YHWH

⁶When Y'hoshua had sent the people away, the people of Isra'el had gone each one to his assigned property in order to take possession of the land. ⁷The people served YHWH through-out Y'hoshua's life and throughout the lives of all the older men who outlived Y'hoshua and who had seen all the great work of YHWH which he had done for Isra'el. ⁸When Y'hoshua the son of Nun, the servant of YHWH died, he was 110 years old; ⁹and they buried him near the boundary of his property in Timnat-Heres, in the hills of Efrayim, north of Mount Ga'ash. ¹⁰When that entire generation had been gathered to their ancestors (died), another generation arose that knew neither YHWH nor the work he had done for Isra'el. ¹¹Then the people of Isra'el did what was evil from YHWHs perspective and served the ba'alim. ¹²They abandoned YHWH the God of their fathers, who had brought them out of the land of Egypt, and followed other gods, selected from the **gods of the gentiles** around them, and worshipped them; this made YHWH angry. ¹³They abandoned YHWH and served Ba'al and the **'ashtarot'(Easter).** ¹⁴The anger of YHWH blazed against Isra'el; and he handed them over to pillagers, who plundered them, and to their enemies around them; so that they could no longer resist their enemies. ¹⁵Whenever they launched an attack, the power of YHWH was against them, so that things turned out badly — just as YHWH had said would happen and had sworn to them. They were in dire distress.

¹⁶But then YHWH raised up judges. ¹⁷Yet they did not pay attention to their judges, **but made whores of themselves to other gods and worshipped them**; they quickly turned away from the path on which their ancestors had walked, the way of obeying YHWH's mitzvot — they failed to do this. ¹⁸When YHWH raised up judges for them, YHWH was with the judge and delivered them from the hands of their enemies throughout the lifetime of the judge; for YHWH was moved to pity by their groaning under those oppressing and crushing them. ¹⁹But after the judge died, they would relapse into worse behavior than that of their ancestors, following other gods to serve and worship them; they abandoned none of their practices or stubborn ways. ²⁰So the anger of YHWH blazed against Isra'el; he said, **"Because this nation violates my covenant,** which I ordered their fathers to obey; and they don't pay attention to what I say; ²¹**in the future**, I will not expel ahead of them any of the nations that Y'hoshua left when he died. ²²This is how I will test Isra'el, to see whether or not they will keep the way of YHWH living according to it, as their ancestors did." ²³**So YHWH allowed those nations to remain where they were**, without quickly driving them out; he did not hand them over to Y'hoshua.

These very nations are the ones attacking Elohim's people today! We are surrounded by them!

We never "**separated**" ourselves, we have forgotten who we are, we have forgotten his torah and consider it foreign, we have forgotten his name, we have assimilated!

But Yah promised to put his Torah in our hearts and cause us to want to do what pleases him (Philippians 2:13 ¹³for Elohim is the one working among you both the willing and the working for what pleases him.)..

And he is doing just that, for about the past thirty years or so his people have been fleeing that old whore mystery religion and turning "back" (Teshuvah) to his Torah. <u>Revelation</u> 17:1, 5, 15, 16; 19:2

<u>Jeremiah 51:6</u>
Flee from Babel (separate yourselves);
Let each one save his life! Don't perish because of "her" guilt.
For the time has come for the vengeance of YHWH;
He will repay her what she deserves.

<u>Revelation 19:2</u>
For his judgments are true and just. He has judged the great **whore** who corrupted the earth with her whoring. He has taken vengeance on her who has the blood of his servants on her hands."

<u>Hebrews 12:14</u>
[14] Keep pursuing **shalom** with everyone and the holiness (**set-apartness**) 'without which' no one will see Elohim.

<u>Romans 6:19</u>
(I am using popular language because your human nature is so weak.) For just as you used to offer your various parts as slaves to impurity and lawlessness (Torahlessness), which led to more lawlessness (Torahlessness); so now offer your various parts as slaves to righteousness (Torah), which leads to being made HOLY (**SET APART**) for Elohim.

TESHUVAH! Listen O Y'srael, turn BACK to YHWH!. . **L.B.**

CIRCLE VERSES: KADOSH (HOLY, SEPARATE)

Exodus 33:16 For how else is it to be known that I have found favor in your sight, I and your people, other than by your going with us? That is what **distinguishes us**, me and your people, **from all the other peoples on earth**."

Exodus 34:15 Do not make a covenant with the people living in the land (**SEPARATE** yourselves) It will cause you to go astray after their gods and sacrifice to their gods. Then they will invite you to join them in eating their sacrifices,

1 Kings 8:53 For you made **a distinction between them** and all the peoples of the earth by making them your inheritance, as you said through Moshe your servant when you brought our ancestors out of Egypt, YHWH Elohim."

Matthew 25:32 All the gentiles/nations will be assembled before him, and he will **SEPARATE** people one from another as a shepherd separates sheep from goats.

2 Corinthians 6:17 Therefore YHWH says, 'Go out from their midst; **separate yourselves**; don't even touch what is unclean. **Then** I myself will receive you.

Revelation 18:4 Then I heard another voice out of heaven say: "**My people, COME OUT of her!**" So that you will not share in her sins, so that you will not be infected by her plagues,

Isaiah 48:20 Get out (**Separate!**) of Bavel! Flee (**Separate**) the Kasdim! With shouts of joy announce it, proclaim it! Send the news out to the ends of the earth! Say, "YHWH has redeemed his servant Ya'akov/Isra'el"

Jeremiah 50:8 Flee (**Separate**) from Babel! Leave (**Separate**) the land of the Kasdim!
Be like male goats leading the flock;

Summary

So here we are at the end of this little book.

* <u>We have learned that the Torah of YHWH</u>: Are his instructions for us to live by **FOOOREVERRRR!** (entire Bible)

* <u>We have learned that YHWH "IS"</u> :

"The Word" (John 1:1) and that "The Word" is his Torah.

"The Word" (Torah) became a human being (flesh) = Messiah (John 1:14)…The walking talking Torah!

* <u>We have learned that YHWH's Torah is:</u>

Truth (Psalm 119:144, 160; John 14:6)

Light (Proverbs 6:23; John 8:12)

Life (Exodus 15:25; John 14:6)

Eternal (Psalm 119:142)

The Way (John 14:6)

Knowledge (Hosea 4:1; Proverbs 8:10, 11:9; Ecclesiastes 7:12) Too many to list here!

Wisdom (Psalm 111:9-10) Too many to list here!

Love (2 John 1:6)

* <u>We have learned that YAH's true people keep the Shabbat</u>: (Hebrews 4:9)

* <u>We have learned that YHWH did NOT send his son to do away with Torah/Himself:</u>

Do NOT think I am doing away with Torah or the Prophets (Mathew 5:17-18; John 1:14)

* <u>We have learned that Torah "still" remains:</u>

(Romans 3:31; 6:12; Mathew 5:17-18; Hebrews 4:9) Way too many to list here!

* <u>We have learned that there are just two categories of people in the world:</u>

Israel and heathens/gentiles (Leviticus 20:26; Deuteronomy 26:19; Mathew 10:5-6; Ephesians 2:11-12) Too many to list here!

Summary

* <u>We have established that YHWH is:</u>
   The Elohim of ONLY Isra'el (over 600 verses confirm this)
   Those who are NOT Isra'el are heathens/gentiles/NOT his people (Ephesians 2:11-13)

* <u>We have learned that IF you obey his Torah with all your heart (with loyalty):</u>
   'Then' you are Isra'el and no longer a gentile (Ephesians 2:19) and many, many more…

* <u>We have learned if you reject Torah:</u>
   You are a heathen/gentile no matter whom you think you are (Isaiah 5:24)
    and even your prayers are an abomination (Proverbs 28:9)

* <u>We have learned that the "Righteous" are:</u> Those who do NOT violate his Torah (1 John 3:4)

* <u>We have learned that the Sabbath still remains:</u>   (Hebrews 4:9, Isaiah 66:23) Well over 200 verses confirm this!

* <u>We have learned that we are to be "SEPARATE" Holy:</u>
   (Numbers 23:8-10)   Too many to list here!

* <u>We have learned only the righteous enter his Kingdom, and the righteous are Isra'el!:</u>
   (Isaiah 45:17; Revelation 12:17; 14:12; Deuteronomy 4:8)

* <u>We have learned that Ha'Satan deceives the WHOLE world!</u>
   (Daniel 7:25; Revelation 13:14; Revelation 18:23)

* <u>We have learned that we are to "know and use" -</u> **HIS NAME** <u>not a Fake name!</u>
   (Exodus 3:15; 9:16; Proverbs 30:4; Ezekiel 39:7) too many to list here!

Dear Reader, if YOUR understanding differs from the Torah of YHWH…then it is this writers' conviction that: <u> 2 Peter 3:16</u> has happened to you and you need to dig and investigate.

AND SO NOW WE KNOW WHAT THE WHOLE DUTY OF MANKIND IS!

ECCLESIASTES 12:13

13 HERE IS THE FINAL CONCLUSION,

NOW THAT YOU HAVE HEARD EVERYTHING: FEAR ELOHIM, <u>AND</u> KEEP *HIS MITZVOT*;

THIS IS WHAT BEING HUMAN IS ALL ABOUT.

ECCLESIASTES 12:13

13 LET US HEAR THE CONCLUSION OF THE WHOLE MATTER:

FEAR GOD, <u>AND</u> KEEP HIS COMMANDMENTS:

FOR THIS IS THE WHOLE DUTY OF MAN.

CONCLUSION

I PRAY THIS LITTLE BOOK has achieved my goal in being 'concise' enough and in stirring YOU the reader to "diligently and sincerely" RUN after YHWH's truth's and to NOT believe a matter just because a so-called Pastor; Minister; Rabbi; or Teacher with certain 'upper-case' letters following their name - tells you…This is the way or that was done away with. NO! You listen to YHWH and HIM alone!

Deuteronomy 32:46-47 (Definition of Life)

[46] he said to them "Take to heart all the words of my testimony against you today, so that you can use them in charging your children to be careful to obey all the words of this **Torah.**
[47] For this is not a trivial matter for you; on the contrary, **it is your life!** <u>Through</u> it you will live long in the land you are crossing the Yarden to possess."

Philippians 2:10-14

[10] that in honor of **the NAME** given Y'shua, **every knee will bow** —
in heaven, on earth and under the earth —
[11] **and every tongue will acknowledge** that Y'shua the Messiah is *Master* —
to the glory of Elohim the Father.
[12] So, my dear friends, just as you have always obeyed when I was with you, it is even more important that you obey now when I am away from you: keep working out your deliverance
with fear and trembling,
[13] for Elohim is the one working among you 'causing you to want to do what pleases him'.
[14] Do everything without kvetching or arguing,

Dear Reader, if you desire to study deeper into the word of YAH, here are but a few sites to begin with:

- www.now-is-the-time.org
- www.wildbranchministry.com
- www.bulldozerfaith.com
- www.lionandlambministry.com
- www.aroodawakening.com
- www.wisdomintorah.com
- www.yashanet.com
- Hebrewnationradio.com

IMPORTANT INFORMATION FOR THE HISPANIC COMMUNITIES: FROM CHILE TO MEXICO

Because there is such a great awakening among the Hispanic communities, I would like to insert some very important information for my Hispanic brethren. . . .

In the "TANAK" Art Scroll series / Stone Edition, on page xix, the following is noted ... (with permission)

This is a 'major' principle in the understanding of history. God 'seems' to slumber, but He 'never' abandons His Master plan for creation. it has been noted that the day after **the Jews were expelled from Spain in 1492.** Christopher Columbus SET SAIL to discover the land that was to become a 'major' refuge and source of support for the Jewish people <u>in the future</u>. It took centuries before this connection became apparent, but the descendants of the despised and tortured Jewish nation would follow in the wake of the explorer who had been commissioned by Ferdinand and Isabella, architects of **the Spanish Inquisition!** (emphasis my own)

<u>F. Y. I.</u> In days of old **Spain** was known as "the land of the Hebrews", hence the name "**Iberia**", the word Iberia means the same as the word "**Eber**" = hebrew ; eber/ia which means "**Hebrew land**".

For this reason the 'oldest' synagogue of 'Europe' is located in **<u>Spain</u>** and the oldest synagogues in the Americas are **<u>Spanish and Portuguese</u>** synagogues! (Sephardic)

The **ancient synagogue of Barcelona** (<u>Catalan</u>: *great synagogue of Barcelona;* <u>Spanish</u>: *Barcelona Mayor synagogue)* Has been described as **the " oldest" synagogue in Europe**. After many centuries of use for other purposes, the building reopened as a synagogue and Museum in 2002. No Congregation prays regularly at the *synagogue*, but is used for festive occasions

Based on this knowledge is the magnificent work being done BY: Mr. DELL SANCHEZ of www.4sephardim.com, this is a wonderful "bilingual" site for further information on this topic.

THE "OLDEST SYNAGOGUES" IN THE AMERICAS:

<u>Brazil</u> - The <u>Synagogue Kahal Zur Israel</u> on <u>Recife</u>, <u>Brazil</u>, erected in **1636**, was the first synagogue erected in the <u>Americas</u>. Its foundations have been discovered recently, and the buildings of the 20th century at the site have been altered to resemble a Dutch 17TH century synagogue.

<u>Jamaica</u> - Synagogue, the first synagogue **<u>Sephardic</u>**, was built in <u>Puerto Real</u> in about **1646**, but was destroyed during the earthquake of **1692**. Another synagogue, the *Neve Shalom synagogue*, was established in "**<u>Spanish Town'</u>**s" monk Street in **1704**, but is now largely in ruins. The only synagogue still in use today, Shaare Shamayim in <u>Kingston</u>, was built in 1912.

Barbados - <u>Nidhe Israel Synagogue</u> in <u>Bridgetown Barbados,</u> : one of the oldest synagogues in the Americas, standing since **1654**, restored and used by the Jewish community in Barbados until this day.

Argentina - <u>Synagogue of the Israelite congregation Argentina</u> in <u>Buenos Aires</u> <u>Argentina</u>, : the oldest synagogue of Argentina, on foot from **1897** until this day.

Suriname - Wood, later brick synagogue *Beracha ve El Shalom* ("blessings and peace") in <u>Jodensavanne,</u> <u>Suriname</u>, built between **1665 and 1671**. Destroyed in 1832, ruins still exist.

- <u>Synagogue Neveh Shalom</u> , erection first completed in **1723** and rebuilt in **1842** or **1843**, currently the only synagogue in use in Suriname.

Curacao, Netherlands Antilles - Jewish community was founded in **1659**. <u>The synagogue in Curaçao,</u> Congregation *Mikvé Israel-Emanuel*, built in **1732**. It is the oldest synagogue <u>still in use</u> today in <u>the Americas</u>. [ ] When the Jews were expelled from the French islands of Martinique and Guadeloupe the number of Jews in Curacao increased and by **1780** reached 2,000, more than half of the white population. The community of Curaçao became the "community mother" of the Americas and assisted by other communities in the area, mainly in Suriname and St. Eustatius. It also financed the construction of the first synagogues in New York and Newport.

St Thomas- The <u>Synagogue of St. Thomas</u> in the <u>Virgin Islands of the United States</u> was founded in **1796**

United States

- <u>Congregation Shearith Israel</u> in New York, **1654**, often called **Spanish and Portuguese** synagogue is the **oldest** Congregation **in the United States.**

- <u>Touro Synagogue</u> The Congregation itself dates back to 1658 when 15 families came **Spanish and Portuguese** <u>Jewish</u>

- <u>Congregation Talmud Torah Adereth</u> the (located on East 29th Street in Manhattan) operates local services since **1863**. The congregation was founded in 1857

- <u>Congregation Mickve Israel</u> of <u>Savannah, Georgia</u> was organized in **1733** by **Sephardic** Jews. The current building of <u>Gothic</u> from 1878 is unique at its plant in the shape of a <u>cross</u>.

Canada - The **Spanish and Portuguese** <u>Synagogue in Montreal</u> is the **oldest** in Congregation Canada

Obadiah 1:20

[20] Those from this army of the people of Isra'el exiled among the Kena'anim as far away as **sefarad**, and the exiles from Yerushalayim in **S'farad**, will repossess the cities in the Negev.

<u>Sefarad/s'farad:</u>   is an 'ancient ' hebrew name for **Spain. (Romans 15:24, 25)**

As Daniel said . . .   **Daniel 12:4** . . . Knowledge shall increase!

To those that may have a bias towards Hispanics, Be careful because There is NO room in YAH's kingdom for such a thing! Yah's people are everywhere!

<u>Genesis 12:3[3]</u>

I will bless those who bless you, I will curse anyone who curses you; and by you all families of the earth will be blessed."

Shalom be with you always! . . . **L.B.**

G L O S S A R Y :

ALEF AND TAV – ALEF is the first letter of the Hebrew alef-bet/alphabet and the tav is the last letter; Translated in most Bibles as 'Alpha and Omega' (Greek)

Antiphonally – music performed by two choirs singing alternate musical phrases.

Artach'Shashta – Artaxerxes, the Persian King.

Astaroth – (also **Ashtaroth, Astarot, Astarte** and **Asteroth**), in demonology, is a Crowned Prince of Hell. He is a male figure named after the Canaanite goddess Ashtoreth.

Avinu – our father.

B'nei – children; sons (as in 'children 'of Isra'el) includes both genders.

Bereshit/bereshis – beginning, translated as 'genesis'.

Botzrah – pen; sheep-fold; enclosure for sheep; fortress.

Chukim – permanent; perpetual regulation.

Cohen – priest

Edom – referring to a person and his ancestral territory S.E. of the Dead Sea, comes from the word ruddy red- akin to the word ADAM.

Efraim/Efrayim – Josephs' younger son and refers to The northern kingdom of Israel- known as the "House of Israel" and referred to as "The Lost ten Tribes" they were separated from the southern Kingdom of Judah, Beyamin and Levi, the southern kingdom is known simply as 'Yahudah '/Judah. Judah is in the land but Efraim (House of Israel are still assimilated amongst the goyim/gentiles/heathen/nations, and most do not know who they are.

Elohei-Tzva'ot – God of armies, usu. Translated as, God of hosts.

Elohim – Almighty one, usu. Translated as GOD.

Emissary – an agent or messenger sent on a mission, esp. one who represents a government or head of state.

Eved – servant; slave.

G L O S S A R Y :

Forever – olam

Gentile – a nation; heathen; pagan Not in covenant with YHWH. 'Goy' in Hebrew.

Ger – proselyte, usu. mistranslated in most bibles as stranger or foreigner. Not easily seen in the English. A convert to the Elohim of Israel.

Goyeem/goyim – gentiles/nations; heathens; pagans.

Ha Shem – the name

Havah/Chavah – Adams ' wife, usu. translated as Eve.

Hebrew – cross-over

Hitgalut – revelation; disclosure.

Iesous – ie = to hail (to salute or honour), sous or sus = zeus (ancient greek deity/god). **Note:** soter = savior, so the correct translation should be iesoter = hailsavior or hail the savior! NOT zeus! (John 5:43)

Ishtar – (Akkadian), Easter in english, Inanna in sumerian, in Mesopotamian religion she is a goddess of war and sexual love. Ishtar is the Akkadian counterpart of the west semitic goddess Astarte.

Kadosh/Kodesh – set-apart; holy

Kippur – cover; atone.

Kvetchin - murmuring; complaining; wining.

Laodicea – luke warm; indifferent

Mishpatim – judgements; rulings.

Mitzvah – command

Mitzvot – commandments

Moedim – appointed times; YHWH's festivals. See: Lev 23 = Yah's calendar

G L O S S A R Y :

Mosheh – Moses.

Mashiach – Messiah; anointed.

Ru'ach – spirit

Ru'ach Ha'Kodesh – The Holy (set-apart) Spirit; spirit of Yah.

Sabbath – see 'SHABBAT'.

Safah berurah – pure lip; pure language

Seh -lamb

Sefarad/s'farad –   an 'ancient ' hebrew name for Spain

Shabbat/Sabbath – from the root word "sabat", literally means to stop, cease, rest…this is why in most translations you will see the word 'rest' in place of 'sabbath'. For Example: Hebrews 4:9
(KJV) There remaineth therefore a rest to the people of God.
(CJB) So there remains a *Shabbat*-keeping for God's people.
(AMP) So then, there is still awaiting a full *and* complete Sabbath-rest reserved for the [true] people of God;

Shaddai – the Omnipotent, usually translated "the Almighty."

Shaw – vain; empty; falseness; worthless.

Shekhem – shoulder

Shem – name

Sh'Khinah – denotes the dwelling or settling of the Divine Presence of God, especially in the Temple in Jerusalem.

Sh'ma – to hear and do. (two things) a verb.

Shomayim / Shamayim - heaven

Teshuvah – to turn away; return; go in opposite direction; usu. translated as 'Repent'.

TNK – TaNaK, an acronym referring to the **T**orah(1st 5 books); **N**eviim (prophets) and **K**etuvim (writings)

Torah – Instruction, teaching, laws, especially those of YHWH, manmade teachings and laws are also called torah, thus causing major confusion in Shául's (Pauls) letters.

G L O S S A R Y :

YAH – Our creators name, erroneously spelled as "Jah" in most 'christian' bibles esp. Psalm 68:4 (5). I say erroneously because the letter "J" did NOT exist in ANY language until about 450 years ago, there still is NOT a "J" sound the Hebrew language.

Yahshua – Salvation/savoiur…literally…"Yah saves"…this is the name of our messiah. Because we do not know the actual 'vowel 'sounds the name is pronounced Yahushua; Yahshua or Yeshua. There NEVER existed a Biblical person named 'Jesus'. Jesus is NOT a translation, because a <u>translation</u> of a word equals the definition of the word being translated; nor is 'Jesus' a transliteration, a <u>transliteration</u> is simply <u>phonetically</u> sounding-out a word of one language with the letters of a different language, causing the transliteration to sound <u>identical</u> to the word being transliterated and 'jesus' sounds nothing like "Yashua".

YHWH – The personal name of our creator, we do not know the exact pronunciation, the most popular pronunciations are: Yaweh; Yahuah; Yahovah or Yehovah. Definitely NOT 'LORD' or Ha Shem!

Yom HaDin – Day of Judgement.

A translation   of a word equals the definition of the word being translated.

A transliteration   of a word equals the 'exact pronunciation' of the word being transliterated, using the letters/alphabet of a different language, causing the pronunciation to sound ' identical' to the word being transliterated.

Transliteration Example: (in hebrew) yud-shin-vav-ayin = Y'shua NOT Jesus, there isn't a 'J' sound in Yashua nor does it end with an 'S' or 'Z' sound as in Jesus! Therefore jesus is NOT a transliteration of Yahshua, jesus is a transliteration of the made-up 'Greek' name 'iesous' except for the 'j' sound which did NOT exist until about 450 years ago the pronunciation is exact!   (iesous/jesus). Nor is the Greek 'iesous' a transliteration of Yahshua, this 'iesous' word ends in an 'S' sound, Y'shua ends in an 'AH' sound.

Translation Example: The word for saviour in Greek is "soter" - Therefore the proper translation for Yahshua in Greek should be 'soter' NOT   iesous' , I don't hear a 'T' or 'R' sound in Iesous! There is no such word 'jesus' in any language that I know of and so that is a fictitious name and has NO definition. It is actually the name given to the ancient 'false' god of the ancient greeks!...Hmmm….

Acts 4:12 (CJB)

[12] There is Y'shua (salvation) in no one else! For there is no other name under heaven given to mankind by whom we must be saved!"

Acts 4:12 (KJV)

[12] Neither is there salvation in any other: for there is **no other name** under heaven given among men, whereby we must be saved.

Gevurot 4:12/Acts 4:12 (OJB)

[12] "And there is no Yeshu'at Eloheinu (God our salvation) in any other, for there is **no other Shem (name)**
under Shomayim (heaven) that has been given among Bnei Adam,
by which it is necessary for you to be spared
[*the Mishpat Hashem in the Yom HaDin*]."(judgement day of YAH))

ONE NAME !!!!!!!!

<u>**MALACHI 3:22**</u>

Remember the TORAH of Mosheh My Servant,

Which I commanded him at Horeb for "ALL" of ISRAEL!

(Notice: Not just for Judah but "ALL" of Israel)

NOTES

NOTES

NOTES

NOTES

NOTES

REMEMBER THE

TORAH OF MOSES MY SERVANT

WHICH I COMMANDED HIM FOR

"**ALL**" OF ISRAEL

MALACHI 3:22

Notice: Not just for Judah, but for 'ALL' of Israel!!